# Right On Target!
## Taking Dog Training to a New Level

Mandy Book and Cheryl S. Smith

Dogwise™ Publishing

Wenatchee, Washington U.S.A.

**Right on Target. Taking Dog Training to a New Level**
Mandy A. Book and Cheryl S. Smith

**Dogwise Publishing**
A Division of Direct Book Service, Inc.
PO Box 2778
701B Poplar
Wenatchee, Washington 98807
1-509-663-9115, 1-800-776-2665
website: www.dogwisepublishing.com
email: info@dogwisepublshing.com

Graphic Design: Shane Beers – Chicago, IL

Photographs by Donn M. Dobkin, Just A Moment Photography,
www.justamomentphoto.com

Illustrations by Judith Winthrop

Cataloging-in-Publication Data is available upon request from the Library of Congress

ISBN: 1-929242-32-8

Printed in the U.S.A.

# DEDICATION

This book is dedicated to "the girls," who are both my pupils and my teachers, and to Tonka, where it all started.

**Mandy Book**

To all my dogs, who targeted on their own many, many times before their dense human figured out what was going on, and to all the dog training pioneers who popularized and refined clicker training and targeting. You know who you are.

**Cheryl S. Smith**

# TABLE OF CONTENTS

# 1

# TARGETING BASICS

If you usually keep dog cookies in your pocket, chances are good that your dog likes to get his nose in, on, or as close to that pocket as he can. That pocket is serving as a target. You've already trained your dog to target on a specific location without even knowing you were doing it! If you've taught your dog to go to his bed or crate when you point to it or tell him to go, that's a target that you trained intentionally. If you crouch down and open your arms wide when you call your puppy, you're using your whole welcoming body as a target. Yet most dog owners don't realize they are using targets in their training.

Think about it. Getting your dog to come to you or go to a specific location on your cue is extremely useful—just imagine all the possibilities! Competitive dog sports usually have a targeting component—over hurdles, through tunnels, in and out of weave poles. Targeting is also useful in day to day situations: Need to get your dog out of the way of approaching toddlers with ice cream cones on a walk? Use your hand as a target to bring the dog to your side, and walk on by.

Large animal trainers must use targeting because you can't just put a leash on a wild animal to get him to move where you want him. Dolphin trainers use targets all the time. Watch a seaquarium show and notice the discs on the ends of poles they put into or hold above the water from time to time. These serve as a target that the animal can go to in order to get a reward. Zookeepers also use targets. They teach elephants to put their foreheads on a target and stay there so it's safer for the keepers to work around them. Chimpanzees are taught to extend an arm to a target so that blood can be drawn or other veterinary procedures can be performed.

Dog owners and trainers can make much more and better use of targets, and we've written this book to do just that. Have you ever wanted to teach your dog to ring a bell when he wants to go outside? Teaching him this skill is teaching your dog to target. Just want to have a dog who behaves well in your home? Use a target to teach him to happily put on a collar, to come when called, to walk without pulling, or to go and lie down. Want to compete in agility? You can use targets to teach the necessary contact zones, the pause table, to get speed over straight lines of obstacles. Rather dance with your dog in canine freestyle? Targets are great for heeling, weaving through your legs, spinning, circling—almost any trick you'd like to have in your routine. Do you think your dog has Star Power? Animals working in commercials or movies use targets all the time—they have to hit a mark, after all. Plus many of the acting behaviors you see on screen can be taught with targets. Targets have nearly unlimited uses!

This Miniature Poodle has been taught to push a toy wheelchair using targets.

## BASIC CONCEPTS

Both of us (your authors) train using a clicker because we have found it to be an extremely effective tool when working with dogs. But some people find it awkward to hold the clicker, present a target, and deliver treats. You can use a whistle, a spoken word (such as "YES!"), or your choice of sound (or, for deaf dogs, a visual such as a pen light). Any of these is a "bridge" or a "marker," which is followed up with a treat to reinforce a behavior you want the dog to perform.

Different choices have different advantages and disadvantages. The clicker is more precise, and not a sound that the dog hears all day, every day. You may feel clumsy with it at first, but it will become more natural with practice, so give it some time. A bridge word is always available to you, and you don't have to hold any extra equipment in your hand, but your dog hears you talking all the time. It's your choice—throughout this book, we will use the generic term "marker" to refer to any sound used to tell the dog "that's it, that's what I want" and you'll either click or say "yes" or some other word you choose.

The marker allows you to break a behavior down into small steps working toward the complete picture—this is referred to as "shaping."

When you start reading the instructions for training a behavior, it may look a bit daunting. All those steps! Keep in mind that training sessions should be very short—certainly no longer than 5 minutes—and you may go through several steps in one session. So two or three sessions a day will allow you to train the easiest behaviors in a day or two. The more difficult behaviors may require you to stay at the same step for several sessions and will obviously take a little longer, but because training sessions will be short, sweet and snappy, both you and your dog should have fun.

We've written the book with two approaches to learning a skill. For our readers who are experienced dog trainers, we give a first set of instructions in outline, or streamlined, form we call "Go." If you're already familiar with clicker training, that may be all you need to get going and train the skill. The second set of instructions, called "Go-The Details," uses the same steps but with deeper explanation to help you overcome any difficulties you may encounter. The "Troubleshooting" section talks about some common and not so common stumbling blocks and how to work through them. The "Keep in Mind" section alerts you to details you will need to pay attention to as you train.

## TIMING

Getting the timing of your marker right is very important—or you risk training the wrong thing! In order to mark the behavior you want, you must be able to time your marker so that it occurs *while* the behavior you want the dog to perform is happening. Many beginners are consistently late in their initial efforts to mark behavior. You can overcome this by doing exercises to improve your timing, without involving your dog. Here are a few:

- While you watch television, choose some common word and click (or say your bridge word) every time a performer says it. Even better, tape shows and try to pause the tape while the performer is saying the word. You know you've got the timing right if you can react quickly enough to stop the tape on that word and not four words later.

- Toss a tennis ball (or have someone else do the tossing) against a sloping surface such as a low roof. Click when the ball hits the roof.
- Toss the ball straight up into the air and click at the highest point of the toss.
- Watch friends play tennis and click each time the racquet hits the ball (the click and "thunk" of the racquet should occur simultaneously).

Now you're getting it!

## BREAKING DOWN BEHAVIORS—YOUR KEY TO SUCCESS

To use a marker to its full potential and develop complex behaviors, you must be able to break the behavior down into small, trainable steps. We have written out the steps for each of the basic types of touches (nose, foot, and body) in the next three chapters. Read over these steps to get an idea of how to break down a behavior. As you follow the steps and gain some experience, you will learn the process of breaking down behaviors so that you can customize this approach to your needs. To help you along, we've broken the early steps down more finely than later steps, and made the instructions for behaviors early in the book more detailed than those coming later.

## CRITERIA

With this kind of training, you need to know when to ask for a little more from your dog. As trainers say, you need to "raise your criteria." Criteria just means the level of behavior you are going to reward. So if you are teaching a nose touch, you might start with the criteria of "dog looks at the target." After your dog does that a few times, you might raise your criteria to "dog moves head toward target," then advance to "dog touches nose to target."

An easy method to use for deciding when to raise criteria is "7 or 8 out of 10 correct." What this means is that in one short training session, you give the dog the chance to do the behavior 10 times. When he gets it right 8 (7 if the behavior is easy) out of 10 times for 2 sessions in a row (just in case it was a fluke the first time), you can then move up to the next step in your training sequence. In the instructions, you'll see the notation "*8 correct? Move up a step.*" We recommend this method as the easiest for those just becoming familiar with mark and treat training.

## REWARDS

Rewards are a kind of paycheck for your dog's good work. He will be investing considerable effort into figuring out what you want him to do, so don't be stingy with your rewards. To avoid loading the dog up on a lot of "fast food" treats, make a click mix by combining a couple of scoops of the dog's dry food with a couple of cups of bite-size treats of cheese or meat (the smellier the better). The treats give a little extra appeal to the dog food by rubbing their flavor onto the kibble, plus the dog never knows what will come out of the treat bag. Store any leftovers in the fridge.

"You want me to do what with this thing?" Don't be stingy with rewards—the dog is working hard to figure out the behavior.

Where and when you give treats can also impact your training. You want to use the delivery of the treat to assist your training, not hinder it. So if you are working on a stationary behavior such as a stay on a mat, give the treat to the dog while he's in the desired position. If you are working on movement, such as a turn to the left, deliver the treat ahead of the dog to encourage movement.

## THE POWER OF OBSERVATION

Even with reasonably good timing, you need to assess your dog's responses on a continuing basis to ensure that the dog is learning what you think you are teaching. You also need to be aware of signs of stress or fatigue—training with a marker encourages the dog to participate fully in the training process, and is mentally tiring. So be a careful observer of your dog's progress. Don't be afraid to take a break.

## RECORD KEEPING AND REVIEWING PROGRESS

Keeping records of your progress will come in handy. We've included a sample record-keeping system in the Resources section of the book. It allows you to track your progress by making just a few marks on a piece of paper. Throughout the book you'll see the notation *"Take a Break, Review Your Progress, Then Resume."* It's our way of reminding you to give yourself and your dog a breather and see that your training is on track. Your break only has to be long enough for you to think back over the session, or check your notes, while your dog relaxes. If your dog seems to be tiring or becoming inattentive, take a longer break. Don't forget to pick up any targets you were working with, so the dog isn't practicing while you take notes!

## IT'S NOT MAGIC! MECHANICAL SKILLS CAN BE LEARNED

As long-time animal trainer Bob Bailey has been heard to say, "training is a mechanical skill." If you're new to this type of training, you'll want to practice your mechanical skills on your own before you bring your dog into the picture. So if, for example, you're going to teach a "touch nose to hand," practice your timing by presenting your hand as a target to an imaginary dog, marking and treating, and removing the target until you can reliably deliver 10 treats in 30 seconds. If you are using a clicker, include the clicker in your practice. Then practice with your other hand as the target, until you can again deliver 10 treats in 30 seconds. Be sure you do not reach for a treat until *after* you've said your bridge (or clicked). When you feel you're ready, go and get your dog.

## USING A TRAINING PARTNER FOR FUN AND PROGRESS

While the majority of people train alone, you'll find working with a training partner is fun and invaluable when problems arise. This gives you another set of eyes and another brain, and can help you past any rough patches. Plan an occasional session with a friend and ask them for feedback.

You won't believe some of the things you don't know you're doing! When you do use video, go ahead and tape entire sessions, but view them in fast forward, so you don't spend half your time in front of the screen. Only view 30 seconds or so out of every 5 minutes and fast forward the rest. You'll still see any glaring errors in your shaping, and the review process will go much more quickly.

## BEFORE YOU BEGIN

We've outlined just the basics of marker and treat training. However, we highly recommend you review a beginner book on clicker training or work with a trainer to help you with the behaviors in this book if you are new to training with a marker. If you are forging ahead on your own, work on the *first* target exercises in each of Chapters 2 through 4 to get familiar with shaping using the "Go— The Details" explanation. These are the simplest to teach, and we will guide you through these behaviors step by step.

Teach only one each of nose, paw or body targets, and then go on to train a target for a different part of the body. If you teach all the nose target behaviors first, you will have a hard time convincing the dog to touch with a foot rather than his nose when you want to move on to other behaviors.

This book presumes that your dog has had some basic training on Sit, Down, Come, Stay, etc. in a group class situation. If you've never attended a class with your dog, we recommend you do that before trying the exercises in this book. It will give you experience with teaching something new to your dog, and let your dog practice learning. If you have used leash corrections to train your dog previously, you may find that he's hesitant to try new things. For more information on introducing such a dog to training using a marker and shaping behaviors, see our book *Quick Clicks* or others listed in the Resource section at the back of the book

We start by teaching the dog how to touch a specific body part to a certain target. For example, you can use your palm and have the dog touch with her nose, use a square of cardboard and have the dog touch it with her front paw, or use a square of material to have the dog touch with her butt. Once these touches are learned you can use them to train a variety of other behaviors. You might transfer the touch to another object, have the dog follow a moving target, or work on duration (how long the behavior continues).

One nice thing about targets is that you can often "leave them in" as part of the end result, such as having the dog lie down on a material square when the doorbell rings or run to touch your hand when he sees another dog approaching. If you do want or need to get rid of the target, fading a target (gradually getting rid of it) is a straightforward process, simple when done at the right place in the training process—we'll explain how to do this later in the book.

## SOME MORE USEFUL DEFINITIONS

Following are some additional terms that we'll refer to throughout the book:

**Bouncing around an average.** The idea that steps in your shaping process should not always get progressively harder. *On average*, you will increase one criterion (either distance, time or number of steps forward) but *each repetition* will vary somewhat around that average. It's usually a good idea to have more repetitions on the low side of the average. So if you wanted to be working at an average of 10 feet away, one repetition might be at 9 feet, one at 14 feet, one at 8 feet, one at 9 feet, one at 7 feet, one at 13 feet, and one at 10 feet.

**Criteria.** A measurement, standard or condition for each step of the behavior.

**Cue.** The word (a verbal cue), hand signal (a visual cue) or other information in the environment (such as an object on the floor) that tells the dog to do a behavior.

**Fade.** The process of gradually getting rid of a now-unwanted cue (a food lure, body language, a target, etc.). For example, most people teach a sit by holding a piece of food (a lure) in front of the dog's nose and moving it up (a visual cue) to position the dog in a sit. As training continues, the food is removed from the hand, then the hand movement is gradually decreased and finally eliminated as the verbal cue is added. The other cues have been faded.

**Generalize.** Teaching the dog to perform the same behavior regardless of location, environmental conditions (presence of other dogs or people), or your orientation, or closeness. You all know the dog who behaves perfectly at home—but the dog who can perform at that same level in any location has learned to generalize.

**Shaping.** A series of steps gradually building a behavior to its final, desired form. The initial steps may only be a small piece of the end behavior, or may not resemble it at all.

# 2

# NOSE TOUCHES

Forgive the pun, but dogs are nosey. They naturally follow their noses to things that interest them. This makes it easy to teach a dog to touch a target with his nose. Nose touches are undoubtedly the most used and probably most useful of the various body touches—you can use your nose targets to work at a distance, practice a variety of dog sports, and teach some cool tricks.

While we cover three nose touch behaviors in this chapter, we recommend you teach only one nose touch initially, and then introduce your dog to a foot and body touch from Chapters 3 and 4, before continuing practice with other types of nose touches. Otherwise, it will be difficult to get your dog to touch with a different body part.

 ## TOUCH NOSE TO HAND

Teach the dog to bump his nose to the palm of your hand. This is an excellent first behavior to teach because you always have the target "handy." Dogs new to target training and/or the use of a marker generally do well with this. It's also a great first behavior for dogs more familiar with other types of training, such as lure/reward or collar corrections. Most dogs like to initiate contact with their humans, so bumping your hand comes easily to them.

## GET READY

This behavior will help you work on your timing, and give you practice using both of your hands. You'll learn how to evaluate your progress, shape your criteria, and add a cue, the word or hand signal that tells the dog to do the behavior. You'll also work on speed and variations in how targets are placed.

We suggest that you start with a hand touch because it's easier for you not to have to fuss with any extra paraphernalia. However, if you're already taught "shake" or "give me your paw" to your dog, it may conflict with the hand touch. You may need to use a separate target in your hand to get the nose touch in that case. See the instructions for targeting on a Contact Disk later in the chapter if this applies to you.

To begin training, you'll need treats and a timer of some sort. If you find it helpful to write things down (we encourage it!) you'll find sample record sheets in the Resource section at the end of the book.

## SUGGESTED CUES

"Touch," "Nose," or "Hand," with your hand held out. Be sure that your verbal cue is very clear to the dog so he isn't trying to do a hand touch any time he wants or whenever your hand happens to be hanging at your side. Once you've added the verbal cue, do not reward any hand touches without the cue word being given first.

## GO!

1. Hold your hand out slightly in front of the dog and wait for the dog to lean or step toward it. Mark and treat.
2. Mark and treat when the dog touches your hand. Continue until the dog is reliably (7 out of 10 tries) bumping your hand when you hold it out.
3. Get the dog to touch both your right and left hands.
4. Get the dog to touch when your hand is held 3 inches lower than his nose.
5. Repeat with the opposite hand.
6. Get the dog to touch your hand when it is held above his nose.
7. Repeat with the opposite hand.
8. Present the hand in different places relative to the dog.
9. Add your cue word.
10. Work in different locations to generalize the behavior.
11. Hold your hand oriented differently (horizontally, with palm up or palm down, for example).
12. Put your hand close to or on different objects at different heights.
13. Teach the dog to respond only when given the verbal Touch cue with your hand held out.
14. Take it on the road (variety and continued practice).

If you run into any problems, see the more detailed training steps at the end of the section in "Go—The Details." Detailed training steps are included with all of the behaviors early in the book, so don't hesitate to refer to them if you need more help.

Start with your hand 6-8 inches in front of the dog for the nose to hand touch.

# KEEP IN MIND

**Don't take the target to the dog.** When you want a dog to touch an item with his nose, don't put the item too close to the dog or he'll tend to actually back away from it rather than move toward it.

**No moving targets.** If the dog doesn't move toward or touch your hand, don't wave it around in front of him to try and get him interested. Instead, put the target behind your back and re-present it. We don't want the dog to think he should only touch the target if it's moving—yet.

**Don't change the rules within a session.** When we start the touch nose to hand behavior, we are really marking "look at or better." If the dog touches each time, he still gets marked and treated. But don't increase your criteria (move to the next step) just because the dog touches with his nose a couple of times. You'll only move up to the next step when the dog is working at 7 out of 10 correct or better for at least two 30 second sessions. Part of the art of shaping is knowing when to move to the next step. Moving ahead before the dog is ready or taking too-large "steps" will be just as inefficient and cause you just as many problems as staying too long at a step.

**Check your timing!** Be sure you mark when the dog's nose touches your hand, *not* as the dog is pulling away or when you deliver the treat. If you're not sure, ask someone to watch you, to be sure your timing is "on." If you need to, practice this step until your timing is accurate. If you are having trouble, ask someone to pretend to be your dog by sporadically touching your hand and giving you feedback on your timing. That way, at least you won't mess up your dog while you're perfecting your timing.

**Time's up!** If you're using a timer to keep your sessions short, do one additional mark and treat after the timer goes off. This prevents the dog from thinking he's "all done" when he hears the timer.

**Bounce around to make it better.** When you start to hold your hand farther away from the dog, it's a good idea not to just continually *increase* the distance between your hand and the dog for each step up in criteria. If you make it increasingly harder every time, some dogs will give up. We want the dog to think that this is a fabulous game to play, and to be willing to keep playing it with you. So you might put your hand 3 inches away for a session, then 8 inches away for the next session, then 6 inches away for a session, then 11 inches away, and so on.

**Say your cue *first*.** When you are ready to add your cue (step 9), it's essential that you say your cue word just before you present your hand, so that the dog begins to anticipate that your hand will appear when he hears the word "Touch." Dogs learn at different rates, depending on past experience, temperament, age, and other variables. Your dog may take a long time to learn a verbal cue, or he may pick it up quickly. As a rule of thumb, it will take about 50-100 pairings of the cue and behavior before the dog starts to understand to do the behavior when he's given the cue.

Mark is too early (before the dog touches).

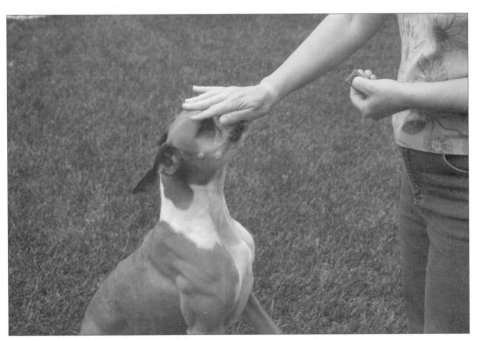

Mark is on time (as the dog touches).

Mark is too late (after the treat).

**Increase difficulty gradually.** Remember to change distraction levels (step 10 above) of your locations gradually—don't work in your living room for one session, then expect the dog to work successfully at the park the next day. An example of this location progression might be :

> 10 varied touches in the kitchen
> 10 varied touches in the living room
> 10 varied touches in the bedroom
> 10 varied touches in the bathroom
> 10 varied touches in the back yard with the dog on leash
> 10 varied touches in the back yard with the dog off leash
> 10 varied touches on the front porch (on leash of course!)
> And so on.

**Mix up your cues to make them more effective.** When you require that the dog touch only when you give the cue word (step 13), the dog may keep trying hard to touch—even if you ask him to Sit. Two things may be going on: he may be really hot to keep practicing Touch because it's been heavily rewarded so recently, or possibly your cue for Sit isn't as strong as you thought. Stop and try a couple of repetitions of Sit and Down (keeping your hands by your side), giving a treat for each correct response. Throw in a Touch, making your hand cue obvious. Practice several sessions while mixing up your cues for Sit, Down, and Touch Nose to Hand, giving a treat for each correct response. Take a short break after every ten behaviors. Keep doing this until your dog is matching the behavior to the cue 8 out of 10 times. Now put your hand up while you say Sit or Down, in such a way that it doesn't look like a hand signal for Touch. For example, flash the hand quickly while you say the word Sit or Down. Reward the dog for the correct behavior. Gradually make your hand presentation more and more obvious as the dog figures out that he should be paying attention to what you say as well as what you do. If you don't take this step to mix things up, the dog will usually try to do the most recent behavior, since it has been well paid. As you teach more behaviors, the dog will learn to pay attention to these cues and it will be easier to incorporate new behaviors into his repertoire.

## TROUBLESHOOTING

*Dog won't touch your hand.*
- Wipe food on your hand.
- Hold the hand farther away from the dog's nose.
- Have someone else try it and watch what they do.
- Videotape to check your presentation and timing.

*Dog won't touch on cue or touches when just your hand (with no cue word) is presented.*
- You trained too long without adding the cue. It can still be done, but it will take longer! For example, Mandy trained one dog to touch only on the hand signal. The dog touched this way for over a year. When Mandy decided to add a verbal cue to the hand signal cue, it took almost 6 months of work. The lesson is, you don't need to get the behavior "perfect" before adding the cue, just "good enough!"

*The dog doesn't have any other behaviors on cue, so you can't work on refining the response to the cue word.*
- Train the dog to Sit and Down on a verbal cue before continuing with this behavior.

## CROSS TRAINING OTHER BEHAVIORS

Transfer the touch nose to hand behavior to other targets, such as a coffee can lid, target stick, or someone's lap. This will enable you to use the "touch nose to item" behavior in a variety of venues, such as agility, freestyle, therapy work, or obedience competition.

Use the touch nose to hand for a distance recall, especially good for dogs who are hard of hearing.

# GO — THE DETAILS

1. Count out 10 treats, and set your timer for 30 seconds. Put your hand about 6 to 8 inches in front of the dog's nose (palm vertical, facing the dog—see photo on page 11), mark and treat when the dog looks at it or sniffs it. Remove your hand after each mark and treat. Repeat until your treats are gone or until the timer goes off. If the timer goes off first, do one additional touch before stopping.

*7 correct? Move up a step. Continue using 7 out of 10 correct for at least two 30 second sessions for the following steps.*

2. Count out 10 treats, and set your timer for 30 seconds. Present your hand, mark and treat when the dog touches it. Remove your hand.
3. Switch hands and repeat the previous step, having the dog touch the opposite hand.
4. Go back to your original hand, and put it closer to the ground, so it is below the dog's nose by about 3 inches, but still with the palm held vertically. Mark and treat when the dog touches your hand.
5. Repeat step 4 using your other hand.

*Take a Break, Review Your Progress, Then Resume*

6. Using your original hand, hold it 3 inches higher than the dog's nose. Mark and treat when the dog touches your hand.
7. Repeat step 6 using your other hand. Continue to alternate your hands, but use the same hand for each 30 second session (each set of 10 treats). We will now raise our criteria to 8 out of 10, so you will move on to the next step when the dog is correct (gets the mark and treat) at least 8 out of 10 tries two sessions in a row. You'll do each step at least twice—once with each hand as the target— and possibly more if the dog doesn't do the required number of touches in the time allotted.
8. Now, vary where you put your hand, keeping roughly the same distance from the dog's head for each touch. So move the hand to your side, to the side of the dog, in front of you, behind you, above the dog's head (so he has to stretch for it), below the dog's head (so he has to hunker down for it). Remember to do this for one session with

each hand. Gradually make it harder and harder for the dog to touch the hand, such as by moving it behind his head or between his legs for the touch, keeping about the same distance within a session, but changing the location each time you present your hand.

Training works best if you change only one thing at a time in each training session, so you want to keep your hand the same distance away from the dog's head while you work on these varied positions.

*8 correct? Move up a step—change the distance of your hand from the dog.*
*Take a Break, Review Your Progress, Then Resume*

9.  Begin to add your verbal cue. Say your cue word ("Touch"), then put out your hand. Mark and treat when the dog touches. Repeat until you have given the dog 10 treats. Vary the distance and the location of the hand relative to the dog. At this point, the dog should have a pretty solid idea of what you want him to do! If the dog does not touch, remove the hand, wait a few seconds, then say your cue and put out your hand again. If the dog still appears to be lost when the hand appears, go back to step 8 until he is successful at least 8 out of 10 tries at a variety of distances and locations.

10. Change training locations and repeat step 9 until you have given the dog 10 treats. Change locations again. For your next training session, find a new location to work on adding the cue. In each new location, repeat until you have given the dog 10 treats. Take a short break, and then move to the next location.

11. Vary the orientation of your hand. Present it horizontal with the palm facing up or horizontal with the palm facing down. Choose one variation to work on in a session, so that you are only changing one aspect each session. Don't forget to use your cue word each time, and to switch hands occasionally. If your dog has difficulty with this step, make the appearance of the hand just slightly different from vertical. In other words, don't start completely horizontal; instead tilt your hand just slightly off vertical, until the dog is successfully touching it.

*Take a Break, Review Your Progress, Then Resume*

12. Vary the relationship of your hand to other objects. Say your cue word and place it against a wall, against the floor, or on top of a coffee table. Mark and treat when the dog touches.

*If your dog doesn't already have Sit, Down, or some other behavior on a verbal cue, train that first before starting the next step.*

13. This step is the difficult part of adding a cue, to teach the dog that he should only touch the hand when you say the cue word *and* the hand is presented and not at any other time. Offer your hand in a difficult position to touch (we want to discourage the dog from touching this time) and simultaneously tell the dog to Sit. If he sits, give him a treat and release him. Chances are that he'll try to touch your hand. If he does, ignore it. Do not mark and treat the touch, no matter how tempting! From now on, the dog is only rewarded for touching when he has both the verbal cue ("Touch") and visual cue (presentation of hand). Wait until the dog stops trying to touch, then tell the dog to Sit again. Let him make a couple of mistakes if he needs to sort this new information out, but don't repeat this over and over if the dog isn't figuring out that he should be sitting and not touching.

14. Present your hand, tell the dog to Sit, and when he sits, immediately tell him to Touch. If he touches, mark and treat. Repeat for 10 treats. On two of the repetitions, reward the dog immediately for a Sit, without asking for a Touch. Working in 10-treat sessions, continue until the dog is doing the correct behavior, in the order requested, at least 8 out of 10 times. Choose another behavior to vary with your Touch, such as Down. Continue to add a variety of behaviors.

We're offering the dog the chance to Touch when he does something else correctly. Using it this way also rewards sitting. Later in the book, when we work on chaining behaviors together, we will use this technique again.

15. Continue to work in different locations, with you facing different directions relative to the dog, with your hand held at different heights and oriented in various ways. Occasionally ask for another behavior instead of Touch. Once in each 10-treat session, do not give the "Touch" cue when you present your hand, then give the cue when the

dog doesn't touch—you are rewarding him with the opportunity to touch after he waits for the cue word.

 # CONTACT DISK

Here, we'll transfer the nose touch behavior to a flat disk, commonly known as a contact disk. The dog will touch his nose to the disk (one or multiple times), without pawing at it, licking it or picking it up. Teaching the dog to touch a target away from your body has a lot of useful applications, such as training agility contacts or the Obedience Go Out or having the dog go to a "station." While teaching this, we'll want the dog to run as fast as possible to touch—we'll achieve that by how we evaluate the steps and by our treat delivery. We'll build speed into the behavior right from the beginning.

## GET READY

If you want to keep track of your sessions (and we hope you will!), you'll need record keeping sheets (see Resouces) different than what you may have used for the touch nose to hand, as now we're counting the total number of responses each session rather than 8 out of 10. You'll also need a timer, and you may find it helpful to videotape these sessions or ask someone to watch you.

As your contact disk, you can use a series of plastic circles starting at about 3 inches in diameter, down to about 1/2 inch in diameter. Or you can simply use a plastic coffee can lid and cut it down as you go or mark it in a bulls eye pattern.

If you want, you can attach the contact disk to your hand using Velcro™ on the ends (to wrap around your hand) and center of a fabric band, and on the contact disk. This may help you manage the clicker, treats, and disk. You can then also use the Velcro™ to attach the disk to objects as a variation. Because we're introducing a new skill (holding the target), you may want to practice holding the target, marking, delivering the treat, and removing the target, until you can do it smoothly, with both hands, 10 times in 30 seconds. Without your dog, of course!

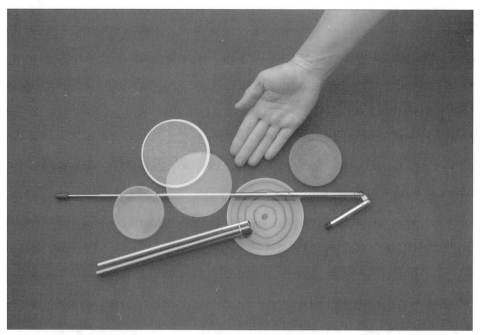

Target options for nose touches.

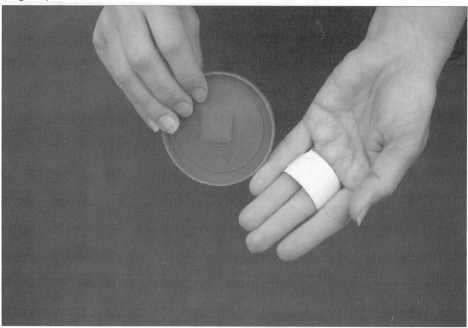

A contact disk can be attached to your hand with Velcro™.

It's essential that you move quickly through the first six steps. If you stay too long at any of these steps, you may convince the dog that the disk should only be touched while it is in your hand. This will be even more likely if you have taught the Touch Nose to Hand recently, or if that behavior is very strong. Remember to switch hands occasionally while working through the first six steps.

Move on to the next step when the dog does 10 touches in 30 seconds or less. This is a different way to assess whether the dog has met your criteria than the 8 out of 10 rule we used in the touch nose to hand. This helps get speed in the process of training the behavior.

After each touch, remove the contact disk, until you get to step 7. This prevents the dog from touching the disk when you're not ready to mark and treat her. Remember to take frequent breaks and to record how many touches the dog is doing in the allotted time to be sure you stay on track.

## SUGGESTED CUES
"Nose," "Touch," "Contact." Make sure it is different from your touch nose to hand cue!

## GO!

1. Hold the disk on its edge. When the dog looks at it, attempts to touch it, or touches it with her nose, mark and treat, delivering the treat on the disk. Remove the disk.
2. Lower your hand so that the disk is below the dog's nose.
3. Continue getting gradually closer to the floor.
4. Touch the disk to the floor, keeping it vertical.
5. Gradually tilt the disk, so it is more horizontal, until it's flat on the floor.
6. Fade your hand out of the picture as quickly as you can.
7. Have the dog touch 1 to 3 times before marking and treating. (Increase your time to 45 seconds.)
8. Place the disk a short distance away. Have the dog wait a second or two, and then release her to touch from 1 to 3 times. Periodically move the contact disk.
9. Gradually build up to least 3 feet away from the disk. (Increase your time to 60 seconds.)
10. Add the cue.
11. Mark and treat only the speediest touches.

12.     Hold the dog's collar, pulling her away from the contact disk. When you feel her pulling forward, say your cue and let go.

13.     Continue to gradually increase the distance until the disk is up to 5 feet away.

14.     Take it on the road, adding distractions and new locations.

## KEEP IN MIND

**Move it around.** Once your reach step 7, you'll no longer remove the disk between touches because that would interfere with getting your hand out of the picture. Now you'll have to be ready to mark and treat if the dog touches the disk, remembering to deliver the treat on the disk. Remove the disk when you are done with your 10-treat session so you can record the amount of time you took without the dog being able to touch the disk.

From step 7 on, you will periodically move the contact disk so it isn't always in the same place in relation to you and the dog. Tossing it (rather than having the dog stay while you place it on the ground away from you) will help keep your dog's motivation to touch it high. Wait a few seconds after you toss the disk to release the dog so that the behavior doesn't become "chase the disk" and so the dog doesn't get the idea that she should only touch it if it has moved. You can also toss the disk behind you, and then turn the dog to face it. Or you can put the disk down, and step away from it.

**Train for speed.** When we increase the distance to the target and the number of touches (step 9), we also increase the time allotment again. However, keep in mind that 60 seconds is just an estimate. You'll have to assess whether this is reasonable for your dog's current physical capabilities. But don't be too generous with your time allotment and train the dog to be unnecessarily slow. Consider how fast your dog could chase her favorite toy—you should expect about that speed touching the contact disk.

If your dog isn't meeting the time allowed, check to make sure that you haven't been working too long, your treats are still valued, there aren't too many distractions, the dog isn't full, etc. If the dog continues to miss the time allotment, it is too difficult for her— increase the time by a second or two and see if she is able to meet that criteria. A good rule of thumb is that the dog can meet the time criteria at least half the time in the initial stages. Decrease the amount of time allotted when the dog is fast enough to get a mark and treat most of the time.

## TROUBLESHOOTING

*The dog appears to give up, lose interest, get distracted, or shuts down or seems frustrated (barking or repeating a behavior that isn't relevant to the one you're working on).*

- Your steps are *too big*. You need to break them down more finely. Making your steps smaller almost always helps solve this problem. Review "Go—The Details" for help if you need to.

*If your dog is slow.*

- The dog has been working too long and is tiring. Take a break and try again later.
- Slowness may have been built into the behavior. If your dog isn't fast when you know she's fresh, you need to make your criteria tougher. Back up a few steps and allow less time for each session. Mark and treat only the touches that are within your allotted time.
- Use really high-value treats (steak, chicken, cheese) so that your dog will keep working even though she may be frustrated. Practice when she's hungry.

*Dog is pawing or biting at the disk rather than touching with her nose.*

- Your mark is probably too late—review your videotape or have a partner observe your session to see if you need to mark earlier. It may help to change your angle of viewing by sitting on the floor so you can see the touch better.
- Try marking before the nose touch to improve your timing and discourage mouthing the disk.

## CROSS TRAINING OTHER BEHAVIORS

A contact disk can be used for obedience go outs, agility contacts, service dogs turning on lights, and a variety of tricks.

## GO—THE DETAILS

1. Put the disk in your hand, either using the Velcro™ band or holding it on the edges with your fingers. When the dog looks at it, attempts to touch it, or actually touches it, mark and treat, delivering the treat on the disk as best you can. Hide the disk behind your back after each mark and treat. When the dog is touching at least 10 times in 30

seconds, move on to the next step. (Continue to use 10 touches in 30 seconds for the following steps.)

2. Lower your hand so that the disk is presented slightly below the dog's nose. Deliver each treat on the disk and remove the disk after each mark and treat.

3. Lower your hand a bit more, getting gradually closer to the floor. Stay at the same height until you get 10 successes in 30 seconds. Then get a little closer to the floor. Remember to deliver each treat on the disk.

*Take a Break, Review Your Progress, Then Resume*

4. With your hand still on the disk, touch the disk to the floor, keeping it vertical. Mark and treat when the dog touches, and remove the disk after each touch.

5. Tilt the disk so that it is more horizontal and you are able to put more of its surface on the floor. Continue gradually putting more of the surface on the floor with each session as long as the dog is successfully meeting your time constraints.

6. Once the disk is flat on the floor, you'll have to fade your hand out of the picture. You'll simply move your hand gradually farther away from the disk. Accomplish this as quickly as you can.

7. Now we'll vary the behavior by having the dog touch multiple times before getting a mark and treat. We are going to increase the time to 45 seconds to account for multiple touches. Decide whether you will have the dog touch 1, 2, or 3 times for each repetition. It may help to plan out a 10-treat session, writing down how many touches the dog will have to do each time before getting a click and treat. Most of the repetitions will require one touch. Only a few of the repetitions will require two or three touches. Remember to deliver the treat on the disk as best you can. Continue at this step until the dog earns at least 10 treats in 45 seconds. Remember she is touching 1-3 times before getting a mark and treat.

*Take a Break, Review Your Progress, Then Resume*

8. Toss the disk or step away from it about a foot. After a brief wait, release your dog to go to the contact disk and touch 1, 2 or occasion-

ally 3 times. Mark and deliver a treat on the disk. Pull the dog away from the disk to a distance of about one foot and release to touch again. Move on to the next step when the dog gets 10 treats in 60 seconds.

9. Toss the disk a couple of feet away, and continue as in step 8. Add another foot when the dog is successful 10 times in 60 seconds.

10. When you are at least 3 feet from the disk, add the cue. Place or toss the disk, say the cue just before the dog does the behavior, then mark and treat after 1 to 3 touches, delivering the treat on the disk by tossing it or following behind the dog. You may need to hold onto the dog to prevent her from diving after the disk—that's a good sign that you're getting speed and enthusiasm with this behavior! Once you have started adding the cue, do not reward any touch that wasn't cued.

*Take a Break, Review Your Progress, Then Resume*

11. Now mark and treat only speedy touches. A realistic time is one repetition in 5 seconds, counting the time it takes the dog to move forward after being sent and our range of 1 to 3 touches each time at a distance of 3 feet. If the dog doesn't touch within the allotted time, cheerfully say "whoopsie" and bring her back to where you started to try again. Usually, the next repetition is faster.

12. If you want to really speed the dog up, you can use the "opposition reflex" to increase her speed. Hold her collar, pulling her away from the contact disk. When you feel her pulling forward, say your cue word and let go. Make sure you don't shove the dog forward or you'll actually teach her to avoid the disk, especially if your dog is a little shy. If your dog doesn't pull forward when held back, take this as a sign that you haven't given enough rewards so far for touching the disk. Go back to step 11 and work through the steps again before moving on.

13. Gradually increase your distance up to 5 feet. Measure it out so you don't go too far, forcing the dog to search for the contact. At 5 feet, you should be able to get a touch in less than 5 seconds with a reasonably fast dog. Review the Touch Nose to Hand instructions for help on increasing distance.

14. Take it on the road to different locations. Use good treats and don't start with too many distractions. Move to a new location when the dog meets criteria in one location.

#  TARGET STICK: FOLLOWING A MOVING TARGET

Here, we'll transfer the nose touch behavior to a target stick and introduce a moving target to the dog. Teaching the dog to touch a moving target has a lot of useful applications, such as training heeling or freestyle moves. The basic process is the same as transferring the touch to a contact disk, with some minor variations. In the initial stages, the dog will be touching the tip of the target stick with his nose, and should not mouth or bite it. In the later steps, the dog will follow the target without actually touching it.

For your target stick, you can use a dowel of 1/4 to 1/2 inch diameter, about 2 to 3 feet long. Paint the tip a different color or push a pencil eraser onto it to help the dog distinguish the tip. Use a rubber band to identify the area which will be marked when touched (anything below the rubber band counts.

You can also get fancy and order a folding target stick or the Click Stick II, a telescoping target stick with clicker attached, from the resources listed at the back of the book.

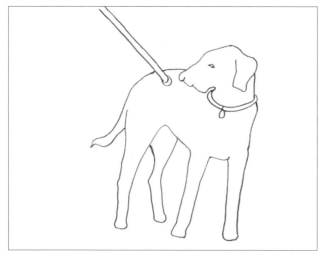

# GET READY

For this behavior, we're going to let you decide when the dog has met the criteria to move on to the next step. That means you can choose to use the 8 out of 10 rule or you can time the number of responses in a 30 second window. For beginners, we recommend the 8 out of 10 rule. More experienced trainers will get excellent speed on a behavior using a "time/number of responses" assessment. To assess a reasonable amount of time for the dog to complete 10 repetitions, time how long it takes you to present the target, click, deliver a treat, and remove the target 10 times—without the dog. Do this with both your dominant and non-dominant hand to get an average response time. If your dog has trouble meeting the time criteria in the early steps (he's successful less than half the time), it may mean that you need to add some time. If he regularly accomplishes the step with time to spare, decrease the allotted time.

Also, the steps outlined here are "lumped" a bit more, so you may need to break them into smaller steps for your particular dog. This will give you practice breaking down behaviors—a necessary skill to be a good trainer.

Unless you've invested in the Click Stick II, which has the clicker built in, there's a bit of skill involved in holding your target stick and a clicker. Brace the clicker on your forefinger, and keep your thumb on the metal clicker, and use your other three fingers to hold the stick. This keeps the clicker off the stick and prevents the vibration of the click from being felt on the target stick (which some dogs find frightening), and leaves your other hand free to deliver treats.

Check to make sure that your dog isn't afraid of the target stick. If the dog seems fearful, spend some time getting him used to it. This is a great opportunity to use a clicker to help the dog overcome his fear of the stick. Start with the stick on the ground, clicking the dog for looking at it, stepping near it, and then touching it. Deliver each treat as close to the stick as you can. Then put one hand on the stick and click and treat for the dog touching anywhere on the stick. Gradually lift the stick from the ground, clicking and treating several times at each change in position. Now you're ready to proceed with training.

*Do not* use a clicker to teach target stick behavior if the dog is also afraid of the clicker. Either use a bridge word or teach the Touch Nose to Hand first with the clicker muffled (in your pocket or with the metal part taped).

Keep these training sessions short, no longer than 1 minute. Set a timer if you need to, so you don't go longer than one minute without a break, or take a 10-second break after each 10 treats, record your dog's progress, and see if

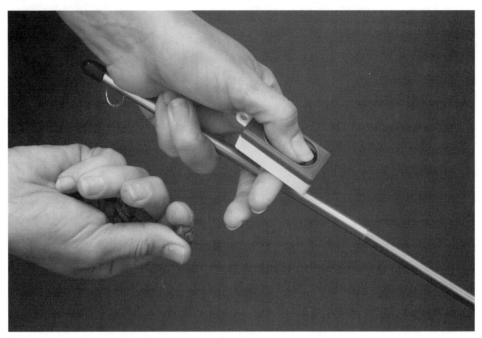

How to hold the target stick, clicker and treats.

he's ready to move to the next step. Take a longer break after 5-7 sessions, to plan your next steps, give you and the dog a mental break, and see how the dog is progressing. Young and inexperienced dogs may need longer mental breaks after a series of sessions.

For each repetition, remove the stick after you have marked and treated, and then present it again for the next repetition.

# GO!

1. Mark and treat when the dog touches the stick anywhere.
2. Using a rubber band to mark the area where the dog has to touch, gradually work the touch to the end of the stick.
3. Present the stick higher, lower, or to the side of the dog, trying to keep the same approximate distance from the dog.
4. Present the stick in front of the dog so the dog has to take a step in order to touch it. At this step, the target stick is stationary when the dog touches it.
5. Add your cue. Do not mark or treat any touches that are not preceded by your verbal cue from this point on.
6. Present the stick a little farther in front of the dog, so the dog has to take several steps in order to touch the end.

7.    Present the stick a couple of steps in front of the dog, and then move it forward as the dog starts to touch. Continue until the dog will take 5-10 steps to touch the end of the stick.

8.    Now mark just before the dog touches the target stick. Continue to vary the number of steps he is taking to follow the stick each time.

9.    Add a variety of distractions and environments for practice.

10.   Add your own movement, so that the dog follows the stick with you moving forward.

11.   Have the dog follow the stick in a circle (you not moving).

12.   Have the dog follow the stick in a figure eight (you not moving).

13.   Fade the target stick to a small piece or just the tip of your finger.

# TROUBLESHOOTING

*Dog bites at the stick.*
- You are marking too late—try to mark sooner, before the dog actually touches. The biting should lessen after a couple of sessions.

*Behavior falls apart or dog stops working.*
- Are your steps too big? That's usually the problem. Try putting 1-2 additional steps between each of the steps you've already outlined.
- Have you been working too long? Maybe the dog is tiring, or is full. Take a break and come back to it another day.
- Have someone watch you, or review your videotape, to make sure your timing is good and the dog is clear what to do to get a click.

# CROSS TRAINING OTHER BEHAVIORS

Use this target behavior to get some very fancy heeling patterns or to tune up any heeling issues. Fade the target stick to your finger or elbow so you have a usable target in the competition ring. The target stick is also great for getting some fancy dance moves—figure 8s, weaving through legs, etc. Use the target stick stuck in the ground to send the dog away from you.

# GO—THE DETAILS

Make a plan for how many steps it will take to get the dog touching the stick and fill in the blank space below with your steps (hint – not many!)

1. _____

2. Mark and treat when the dog touches the stick anywhere. Deliver the treat at the end of the stick.

*8 correct? Move up a step (and continue to use 8 out of 10 correct for the remaining steps).*

3. Use the rubber band to mark an area at least 5 inches below where your hand is on the stick. Mark and treat for touching anywhere below the band. Deliver the treat at the end of the stick. Remove the target stick after each mark and treat.

4. Roll the rubber band down 2 inches. Mark and treat for touching anywhere below the rubber band. If the dog is biting at the stick rather than touching with his nose, have someone watch you, or review your videotape. You probably need to mark sooner.

*Take a Break, Review Your Progress, Then Resume*

Make a plan for how many steps it will take you to get the rubber band all the way to the bottom of the stick with *this* dog and fill in the blank with your steps.

5. _____

6. Continue marking and treating below the rubber banded area, until you have moved the rubber band all the way to the end of the stick. Remember to deliver the treat at the end of the stick on every repetition, regardless of where the dog touched the stick.

7. Remove the rubber band and mark and treat only touches on the end of the stick.

8. Present the stick higher, lower, or to the side of the dog, trying to keep the same approximate distance from the dog. Mark and treat when the dog touches the end of the stick and deliver the treat at the end of the stick. Remove the stick after each repetition so the dog can't touch it when you aren't prepared to mark and treat the behavior.

*Take a Break, Review Your Progress, Then Resume*

9. Present the stick in front of the dog so the dog has to take a step in order to touch it. Mark and treat when the dog touches the end. For this step, the target stick is stationary when the dog touches it.

10. Add your cue. To add the cue, say your cue word, present the target stick, mark and treat when the dog touches the end, then remove the target stick. Do not mark or treat any touches that are not preceded by your verbal cue from this point on. You can use the same cue as for your Touch Nose to Hand behavior, if you like. Here, the dog is still touching something attached to your body. With the contact disk, we changed the cue because the dog was touching something apart from your body.

11. Present the stick a little farther in front of the dog, so the dog has to take several steps in order to touch the end. The stick will still be stationary when the dog touches it. The sequence is: say your cue, present the stick, mark and treat for touching the end, remove the stick.

12. Say your cue, present the stick a couple of steps in front of the dog, and move it forward as the dog starts to touch. Mark and treat when the dog touches the end. The dog now has to follow and touch the target stick while it is moving. Don't make it too hard for the dog to touch the moving stick initially. We've just changed the picture by having it become a moving target, and we want the dog to continue to be successful so we don't lose the behavior.

*Take a Break, Review Your Progress, Then Resume*

Make a plan for getting the dog from following a moving target one step, to following it 5-10 steps before touching it. Here's a hint—don't just gradually add more and more steps. Remember how we added one to three nose touches in the contact disk work? You'll use the same idea to get the dog to multiple steps. There have to be more repetitions at fewer number of steps than at many steps, especially in the early stages. If it just gradually gets harder, the dog may stop working.

13. When you have the dog following the target stick and touching it while it is moving, and he will take up to ten steps following it, we will change to marking *just before* the dog touches the target stick. Continue to vary the number of steps he is following the stick each time. This step allows us to fade the target stick easily and to move the target faster to get speed out of the dog as needed. A 10 treat sequence might look like: 4 steps, 2 steps, 8 steps, 4 steps, 1 step, 5 steps, 3 steps, 7 steps, 2 steps, 4 steps. In that sequence, the dog is taking on average 4 steps before getting a reward. The remaining steps are variations working with this behavior. Be sure to list out all the individual steps you'll need to take to accomplish each of these variations with your dog. Remember to break each of them into a series of small steps that are achievable with your dog. Record your progress, and use your 8 out of 10 rule so you know when to move to the next step.
14. Add a variety of distractions and environments for practice.
15. Add your own movement, so that the dog follows the stick with you moving forward.
16. Have the dog follow the stick in a circle (you not moving).
17. Have the dog follow the stick in a figure eight (you not moving).
18. Fade the target stick to a small piece or just the tip of your finger.

# 3

# FOOT TOUCHES

Some dogs are very foot oriented and some are not. If your dog holds toys between his paws, paws at you when he wants attention, pounces on things with his front feet, or rears up and spars foot-to-foot with other dogs, teaching foot touches should be easy for the two of you. With dogs who rarely use their feet, or may even seem unaware that they have feet, you'll have to work a little harder.

In this chapter, we'll start with a front foot touch, working on duration (staying on the target), and decreasing the size of the target. Then we'll offer a variation, a foot swipe rather than a solid touch. You can work either variation as your first foot touch.

## TOUCH FRONT FOOT TO TARGET

The object is to have the dog place either front foot on a flat target. The target may be on the ground or oriented in other positions. This is a good choice for sending the dog away from you and having him perform behaviors at a distance. It's a good follow-up to a nose touch, to help the dog understand that touches with different body parts will be rewarded.

## GET READY

If you have just completed working on one of the nose touches, you may find that the dog will offer nose touches to the new target. You will have to let the nose touches go unrewarded until they stop, in order to achieve the foot touch.

Wails of protest from those who've just worked so hard to get a good, reliable nose touch! But stop and reflect a moment. Your targets will be completely different. And your nose touch should be *on cue*, meaning the dog shouldn't be rewarded for offering uncued nose touches anyway.

If you're concerned about keeping your nose touch behavior intact, you can use a separate training session, in a different location, with a different target, and your verbal cue, to reinforce nose touches. Use it to your advantage by mixing in nose touches with other behaviors you have on cue, and be careful not to reward uncued behaviors.

Make sure that your foot touch target does not resemble your nose touch target. So if you used a plastic tub lid for a nose touch, don't use another plastic lid for a foot touch. A piece of cardboard can be cut down little by little as you practice. Carpet or stiff material squares in progressively smaller sizes work well if you have access to them. Strips of painter's tape work well on hard surfaces.

Training an agility contact using a front foot touch on a square of carpet.

You'll also need treats and a timer of some sort, and you'll find a record sheet helpful (see Resources for some examples). Practice your mechanics before beginning (see Chapter 1).

## SUGGESTED CUES

"Foot," "Hit It,'" "Go Out," or "Push." Be sure this cue is distinct from your cue for nose touches. So you wouldn't use Nose for that and Toes for this, for example.

## GO!

1. Put the target on the floor in front of your dog and mark and treat for any interaction with it other than a nose touch.
2. Mark and treat when either of the dog's front feet touch the target. Remove the target after each treat.
3. Put the target to the side a bit. When the dog puts either front foot on it, mark and treat.
4. Vary the position again, at the same distance. Continue changing the placement of the target at every session.
5. Work on duration. Mark and treat several times, before the dog moves off the target.
6. Delay the mark/treat a little each time, gradually increasing the time, until the dog will remain on the target for 10 seconds for one mark/treat.
7. Add your verbal cue.
8. Work on distance, gradually standing farther away from the target.
9. Mix up your cue for "Foot" with other cues such as Sit and Down.
10. Gradually change the orientation of the target as needed.
11. Decrease the size of the target gradually until it is as small as you want it to be.
12. Take it on the road (variety and continued practice).

## KEEP IN MIND

**Watch that timing!** Try to anticipate the foot touch, so your mark will be properly timed with the dog touching rather than removing the foot. Look for precursors to the foot touch, such as the dog leaning or reaching forward. You want to be sure to mark when the dog puts a foot on the target, *not* as he picks the foot back up. The dog should connect solidly with the target, not hover around it or pull back from it.

**Keep the behavior going.** By delivering multiple mark/treats with the dog in position, you are building duration into the behavior. If you marked and then had the dog run to you for the treat each time, you would later have trouble convincing the dog to stay on the target. Rewarding on the spot, especially getting in multiple rewards, and then using a clear release cue (a cue that tells the dog he's done with the behavior) will help you develop a dog who targets and stays at the target, awaiting further instructions. Remember, each time you mark, you will deliver a treat.

**Bounce around.** Use your "bouncing around" technique (see Chapter 2) to vary the number of mark/treats you deliver for each repetition as you build on duration. One way you can help yourself do this is to roll a die before each repetition and try to deliver that number of mark/treats to the dog on the target before releasing the dog.

Saying "one ba na na" to yourself gives you four approximately 1/4 second beats you can use for timing. As long as the dog is successful (that is, waits on the target for the mark/treat) 8 out of 10 times, you can increase the delay *between* each mark and treat. Remember to call the dog to you for the final treat each time.

**Put it on cue.** The cue word must send the dog to look for and touch the target, no matter where it is. Once you have a behavior on cue, do not mark and reward if the dog moves to touch the target before he is cued. Call the dog back to you to wait for the cue. It is not just the visibility of the target, but the verbal cue itself, that needs to trigger the behavior.

# TROUBLESHOOTING

*Dog will only touch the target with his nose.*
- You worked a lot on nose touch behaviors, and didn't wait for nose touching to stop when you started working on a foot touch. Mark anything other than an attempt to touch with the nose and feed above the target rather than on it. Have a training partner help with observation and timing, if necessary.

- Place the target so that the dog can only touch with his foot, such as under a folding chair.

*Dog runs to the target as soon as he sees it, without a cue.*

- You waited too long to add the cue. Practice position cues—Sit, Down, Stand—so they are very strong, and work far from the target at first, gradually moving closer. When the dog will perform positions reliably near the target, go to step 12.

# CROSS TRAINING OTHER BEHAVIORS

Being able to send your dog to a mark and then have her perform behaviors is essential for movie work (see Chapter 9). What other ways might you be able to use a foot target, or a foot movement you could get with a target? Think conformation and the stacked pose, freestyle high-stepping moves, the flyball box, or agility contacts. For some behaviors you may need to elevate the target or decrease the size of the target if you haven't already done so.

Take a good look at the dog skateboarding on the cover. The skateboard behavior was taught with a foot target, starting with one foot, then adding a second and a third, then carefully adding movement. You, too, could have a skateboarding canine, and here's how to do it:

## BONUS BEHAVIOR — SKATEBOARDING!

1. *Start with a skateboard with the wheels removed, or use telephone books on either end to prevent it from moving. Teach the dog to put a front foot on the board or use a previously trained foot target secured to the skateboard.*

2. *Add the other front foot, then a back foot if you wish. Large dogs have an easier time with just their front feet on and pushing with the back feet.*

3. *Working on carpet, remove the telephone books, and mark and treat any movement of the skateboard when the dog gets on, with the correct number of feet on the board. Make sure the dog will be okay with a moving skateboard before working on this step!*

4. *Mark and treat only forward movement, gradually increasing the distance. An easy way to get forward movement is to start with the dog behind the skateboard and let her run toward it*

*to put her feet on it. You will automatically get board movement.*

5.   *Move the board to a less resistat surface such as a kitchen floor.*

# GO—THE DETAILS

1.   Count out 10 treats and set your timer for 60 seconds. Put your target on the floor in front of the dog. If your dog tries to nose touch the target, ignore it. Wait for any behavior *other than an attempt to touch with the nose*. Mark it and deliver the treat above the target. Take a 10 second break to reload treats after your timer goes off. Continue at this step until the dog attempts to touch with her nose (i.e., makes an error) less than 20% of the time.

2.   Put your target down in front of the dog. Mark and treat when either of the dog's front feet touches the target, and deliver the treat at nose level over the target (rather than directly on the target). Pick up the target after each treat. Repeat until your treats are gone or the timer goes off.

*7 correct? Move up a step.*

3.   Place the target in a slightly different position relative to the dog. So if you had put the target directly in front of him, now put it off to one side a little bit. Continue to mark when either front foot touches the target (or whichever foot you've chosen if you're working only one foot), to reward over the target, and to remove the target between repetitions. *Hint:* It's easier for a beginner to mark a specific foot touching rather than either foot.

*8 correct? Move up a step. (Continue to use 8 out of 10 for the following steps.)*

4.   Move the target to a different position and repeat step 3.

*Take a Break, Review Your Progress, Then Resume*

If you wanted to work on a foot swipe rather than a solid touch, you would begin that here (see the next behavior).

5.  Now begin to work on duration, or the length of time the dog holds his paw on the target. Increase your sessions to 2 minutes. Mark when the dog's front foot touches the target, and deliver the treat to the dog. If you can, mark and treat again before the dog moves his foot off the target. Mark and treat a third time if the dog is still in place on the target. Use your release cue word (this tells the dog he can move and is commonly used in teaching Stays) to end this repetition, and call the dog to you for a treat (no mark needed). You will no longer remove the target between repetitions. Be prepared, however, to mark and treat when the dog touches, because the dog will be ready to work. We don't want any correct foot touches to go unrewarded at this point, so you may have to hold on to the dog or pick up the target between sessions.

*Take a Break, Review Your Progress, Then Resume*

6.  Now work on solidifying duration. You don't want to have to keep marking and treating to keep the dog on the target, so you'll have to start reducing the number of mark/treats. Put your target down, and when the dog touches the target, delay your mark for half a second. Mark and deliver a treat, then delay the next mark/treat. Vary the number of mark/treats you deliver for each repetition, delaying each mark just slightly. If your dog leaves the target, or starts trying to do something else when you start delaying the mark and treat, you are waiting too long before marking. Shorten your delay. So you might start with: Dog touches target, you count "one," mark and give a treat, count "one," mark/treat, count "one," mark/treat, release dog. Then increase the delay to "one ba" before delivering the mark/treat. And so on, remembering to be variable a bit, and not just continually increase the amount of time (or do the same number of mark/treats each time!). So your next session might go back to "one" before marking and treating, then a session of "one-ba-na", then a session of "one-ba". (See Keep In Mind for more tips.) Extend the delay, gradually delivering fewer mark/treats, until the dog will remain on the target for up to 10 seconds for one mark/treat.

*Take a Break, Review Your Progress, Then Resume*

7.  Begin to add your verbal cue. Hold onto your dog, say your cue word ("Foot"), and release your dog. Mark and treat when a front foot touches the target. Continue to give multiple mark/treats (from 1-3) while the dog is on the target. Release and call the dog to you for a final treat so that you can reset and send the dog again. If the dog does *not* move to touch the target when cued, pick up the target. Wait a few seconds until the dog stops trying to do anything, then put the target down and say your cue. If the dog still appears lost, go back to step 5 and work up to this step again, working more sessions at each step.

8.  Now, continuing to mark/reward multiple times, begin to work on distance. Stand a couple of feet farther from the target with your dog. Say your cue and let go of the dog. Mark when a foot touches the target and remains there for your required amount of time. Release and call the dog to you for a final treat each time. If the dog is responding quickly to your cue each time, gradually increase the distance, bouncing around at different distances each session.

*Take a Break, Review Your Progress, Then Resume*

9.  Mix up your foot touch cue with other cues that your dog knows. Stand a considerable distance from the target, facing sideways to it (we want to discourage the dog from touching this time). Tell your dog to Sit, Down or Foot, and reward each correct response. Take a short break after every 10 behaviors. Move gradually closer to the target, and keep mixing up the cues and getting correct responses. You're helping the dog to figure out he has to pay attention to what you say even when the target is in the picture.

10. If you need to have the target oriented other than flat on the ground, introduce that at this step. You will gradually, over the course of several sessions, make the presentation of the target closer to your end goal.

11. If you are planning on making your target smaller, now would be a good time to do that. Use your smaller and smaller rug samples, or cut down your cardboard rectangle a little at a time. Work with each new size target, varying the distance and the duration, until the dog is correct at least 8 out of 10 times. Then go to the next smaller size. A good rule of thumb is about an inch smaller in diameter for each step. But you may have to adjust for your dog. There will also be a limit

to how small a target the dog can find without spending a lot of time searching for it.

12. Change your training location and do 8 foot target behaviors, varying the amount of time the dog must stay on the target, and mix in 2 other cues such as Sit or Down. Change locations again. For your next training session, find three new locations to work in. In each new location, follow the same 10-behavior procedure. Take a short break, then move to the next location. Remember to continue to vary the time on the target and to release the dog or call him to you when you want him off the target. Change distraction levels of your locations gradually—don't work in your living room for one session, then expect the dog to work at the park the next.

 ## FRONT FOOT SWIPE

The object is to have the dog paw at a target with a front foot. It's a moving behavior, so it can challenge your timing a bit more. Be careful that your target does not resemble anything your dog will commonly see in your house, or you could end up with scratched walls or cabinets!

## GET READY

It will help to know what your dog looks like when he paws, so take every opportunity to observe any pawing behavior. Pay special attention to any precursors, such as shifting weight, lifting a foot, etc.

You have two basic choices regarding type of target. If you use something like a carpet square, you will spend a certain amount of your training time chasing the target around the room. But the motion may encourage your dog to paw more and harder. If you use tape as a target, it's more likely to remain in place, at least most of the time, but it may be more difficult to encourage your dog to paw. We suggest you use a target square of some kind and if chasing it around gets to be too much, lightly tape it down.

Target options for foot touches.

## SUGGESTED CUES

"Swipe," "Toro," "Scrape."

## GO!

(For steps 1 through 4, see Touch Front Foot to Target.)

5. Raise one side of the target so it is up off the floor at an angle. Continue gradually raising it until the target is vertical.

6. Lean or tape the target to a wall. Mark and treat when the dog moves his foot a small amount.

7. Continue to increase your criteria little by little until the foot swipe looks the way you would like it to.

8. Mark and treat multiple foot swipes.

9. Bounce around 3 foot swipes, doing more easy than hard repetitions.

10. Add your verbal cue.

11. Work on distance from the target, increasing it gradually.

12. Mix up your "Swipe" cue with other cues.

13. Make the target smaller, as needed.

14. Take it on the road.

# KEEP IN MIND

**Picture the performance.** Working on this behavior will require you to observe more closely and keep the behavior you will accept (the level of behavior that will be marked and treated) at each step clearly in mind. Remember that for *your* dog, the difference in touches may be very subtle. To be able to shape the swipe, you may start with an almost imperceptible foot movement. Reviewing video, or having a helper will be invaluable in the early stages. It may help to have a small bit of tape next to the target marking the minimum range of acceptable swiping. Remember, anything at that level or better counts! If your dog suddenly offers a brilliant, picture-perfect foot swipe, do not immediately raise your criteria and wait for an equally brilliant repetition. Your criteria remain the same within a session, and you mark and reward any repetition that meets or beats the set criteria.

**Move your target.** Also, experiment with where you put the target. You may get more (or less) "swiping" movement if the target is angled differently, on the floor, or higher on the wall.

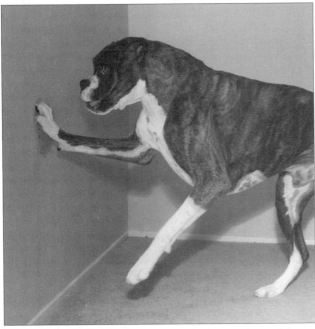

Putting the target on the wall may help get the swiping motion.

**Random rolls.** If you need help with being random when you start to require multiple swipes, take a small box. Write "1" on 2 sides, "2" on 2 sides, "3" on 1 side, and "4" on 1 side. Roll the box before each repetition and do the number of swipes indicated.

**Choose one for best success.** If you are new to clicker training or using a bridge word, it will be difficult to train both a foot swipe and a solid touch, but it is possible if you want to challenge yourself. Pick the one you think you'll be most likely to use (a swipe or solid touch) and train that first. Once you have experimented with touches with other body parts, come back and train the other variation.

## TROUBLESHOOTING

*The dog doesn't move a foot.*

- First, you need to observe more closely. The dog *has* to move a foot in order to touch. You may need to click the beginning of that movement to get a bit of a behavior you can shape into the swiping motion.
- Second, you can encourage the dog to make a swiping motion by taping the target higher on the wall, so the dog has to reach up higher to touch it. Raise the target little by little, then be prepared to mark while the foot is moving. The dog is unlikely to hold his foot stationary in a high position. Once you have marked the foot movement for several sessions, you can lower the target again and the dog should keep offering movement, now that it has been rewarded. (Caution: the wall behind the target may suffer scratches.)
- Make the target easy to move on the floor. It makes it easier for you to see what is happening (the whole target moves) and the movement may encourage the dog to offer stronger behavior.
- Don't mark every touch on the target. If the dog has been getting regular rewards for a touch, and you stop marking and treating touches, he will alter what he is doing. When the soda machine doesn't deliver a soda after you put in your money, most people bang on the machine or do something else before putting in more money! Do a couple of sessions of marking 1, 2, or 3 touches in a row. This will give you some variability in how the dog touches. Also, as the dog learns that this is part of the game, it will be easy to get more varied types of movement.

# CROSS TRAINING OTHER BEHAVIORS

This behavior is most useful as something you can transfer to other objects. So, you could target the dog to a light switch and use the swipe to turn it off. You could target the dog to a ball and have him hike the ball between his legs or roll it with one foot. You could target to a cabinet door and use the swipe to push the door closed. This "scratching" behavior is sometimes specifically requested for movie work, and you'll have it on cue!

## GO—THE DETAILS

For steps 1 through 4, see Touch Front Foot to Target.

5.  Vary the position of the target so that one side is slightly angled up off the floor. Mark and treat each foot touch, and remove the target after each treat.

6.  Continue to gradually increase the angle until the target is vertical and you can tape or tack the target to the wall. Continue to mark and treat for a touch with either front foot. Remember, you won't change the angle until the dog is correct 8 out of 10 times, and each change will only be slightly different from the last position.

7.  Lean or tape the target to the wall. Start by having the dog touch 2 or 3 times before getting marked and treated. You will see a lot of variability in the touches this way, and will be able to start to pick out "scrapes" from "touches." Repeat for several sessions.

8.  You will only mark and treat moving touches now, so not every touch will be rewarded. Your criteria will be a little more subjective. Have a picture in mind of what a slightly improved foot swipe will look like. If the dog is touching only the bottom edge of the target, maybe you want a higher start. Or if the dog is reaching high to touch but then freezing, you may want an additional inch of movement downward. With your criteria in mind, mark and treat only those efforts that meet or exceed your requirements. Then gradually increase your criteria, little by little. When the dog successfully meets the new criteria, move up a step until the foot swipe looks the way you would like it to.

*8 correct? Move up a step. (Continue to use 8 out of 10 for the following steps.)*

*Take a Break, Review Your Progress, Then Resume*

9. Wait for multiple foot swipes. Do not mark and treat the first swipe. Alternate between one and two swipes for ten repetitions.

10. Bounce around three swipes, generally doing more "easy" (one or two swipes) than "hard" (three or four swipes) repetitions.

*Take a Break, Review Your Progress, Then Resume*

11. Add your verbal cue. Say your cue ("Toro") and mark and treat when he swipes the target between 1 and 3 times. From now on, do not mark and treat if the dog touches the target without a verbal cue.

12. Work on distance. Stand slightly farther from the target. Say your cue and mark and treat varying multiples of swipes. Over the course of several sessions, you will increase the distance, remembering to bounce around at different distances rather than steadily increasing the distance. If the dog has difficulty at a longer distance, a good rule of thumb is to decrease it by 20% for the next session, then build distance more gradually.

13. Check that your dog is learning to discriminate this cue from other behaviors and that he will only touch the target when you say the cue word, by mixing up your swipe cue with other well-known cues.

*Take a Break, Review Your Progress, Then Resume*

14. If you are planning on making your target smaller (fading it), now would be a good time to do that. See the previous behavior for more information on how to do this.

15. Change your training location. Continue to vary the swipes on the target. Occasionally ask for another behavior such as Sit or Down. Remember to change distraction levels of your locations gradually—don't work in your living room for one session, then expect the dog to work at the park the next.

# 4

# BODY TOUCHES

In this chapter, we'll move away from the obvious nose and feet to more unfamiliar body parts. The easiest touch here is the first, a full-body touch on a large target. Then we'll introduce a hip touch. This can be difficult for beginner dogs and trainers. Dogs, as a rule, aren't aware of a lot of their body parts, or even whether they're moving them. The rear quarters can be particularly problematic.

Also, these touches are most useful when they're sustained. So training duration will be one of the criteria, and it can be difficult to shape. Finding a way to get the dog to start a behavior involving other body parts can also be a challenge, so we have some suggestions for you.

 ## ON YOUR MAT

The dog will go a distance away and lie down on a mat—a full body touch—until released. You can teach the dog to automatically lie down when he reaches the mat (the easier behavior and the one we'll describe) or to do something different each time based on a second cue given after the dog is on the mat.

## GET READY

This is a great skill for the dog to have at home—teaching them to lie down while you are eating, when someone knocks at the door, or while you are visiting friends. We'll be using it primarily in the house, so it's very quick to teach because it doesn't require a lot of generalization. It also has applications in more advanced work such as agility, where a dog goes to a table and does a Sit or Down, or the Obedience Go Out, where the dog runs to the edge of the ring, then turns and sits when told.

Use a towel, bath mat, or small blanket for a target. In the initial steps, use the same mat. You can generalize to any large, flat piece of material on the floor once the dog has the concept, in later steps. You'll also need a single die, and a timer so you don't work too long. Before starting with the dog, practice rolling the die, then counting that number of seconds before marking and treating. Can you get ten repetitions in one minute? Then you're good to go with the dog!

If you haven't taught the dog a release cue (meaning she doesn't have to be on the mat any longer), you'll need that for this behavior. Any basic book or beginner class will review a release cue when describing how to teach a Stay.

If the dog is very strong on his foot and/or nose touches, you may have to extinguish those in the early stages. See Troubleshooting for more information.

## SUGGESTED CUES

"On Your Mat," "Time Out," "Hang Loose," "Penalty Box," "Go To Bed."

## GO!

As a preliminary step, practice putting the mat down and marking and treating the dog for any interaction with the mat—sniffing, touching or stepping on it. Try this while watching TV during commercial breaks, then pick up the mat. After a couple of days, the dog will be very eager to get to the mat.

1.    Mark and treat for stepping on the mat.
2.    Mark and treat for sitting on the mat.
3.    Mark and treat for lying down on the mat.
4.    Add a cue word (and hand signal, if desired).

5. Increase time on the mat.
6. Continue to add duration until the dog will stay on the mat up to 5 minutes.
7. Add distance from the mat.
8. Add distractions in the house.
9. Take it to other locations.

## KEEP IN MIND

**Use a release.** If the dog doesn't get off when you release him, clap your hands or do something else to get him to move off the mat. He may not want to get off if you did your preliminary homework well! But we want to be very clear when it is okay to leave the mat, and when he needs to remain on the mat.

**Keep it short!** Many trainers work too long, without considering how difficult the work is for the dog. A young or novice dog may tire easily and it's best to come back to the training another time. It's human nature to want to keep working until things improve. It's also human nature to want to continue if things are going well, sometimes until they fall apart! But it's a common fallacy that you should end the training on a good note. Our personal experience is that if things aren't working, you should stop the session and re-evaluate what you're doing. Since the trainer is "driving," the dog shouldn't have a clue if things are going wrong. It doesn't matter at all to the dog how it ends—as far as he knows, it's all good if treats are involved. So it's not necessary to "end on a good note"— sometimes it's a good idea just to "end."

**Give the dog a bone.** It can help build up duration (the length of time the dog remains on the mat) if you give the dog a chew bone or something to do while he hangs out on his mat. Take it up when you release him. We want the mat to be a great place for him to be!

## TROUBLESHOOTING

*Dog paws or bites at the mat.*
- This can be frustration, or previous training may be interfering with the mat work. Use a clicker to more precisely mark going to the mat, clicking before the nosing, biting or paw swipe.
- Change the mat to a stiffer or heavier material. Have the dog lie down immediately, treat and release.
- Tape the mat to the floor in the beginning stages.

- Ignore the pawing or biting, then mark and treat when it stops.

*Dog won't go to the mat.*
- Use a treat as a lure. Toss the treat to give a hand signal.
- Make sure the dog gets lots of repetitions at short distances with a treat on mat.

You can toss a treat and incorporate an arm signal at the same time.

*Dog chews or rips up the mat.*
- Give the dog something else to do on the mat (a Kong™ or other chew toy).
- Try a different material as your mat.
- Don't leave the mat down when you are not supervising or working on the behavior.
- Come back to this behavior when the dog is older and less interested in chewing on novel items.

*Dog won't stay on the mat.*
- Build up duration using bouncing around rather than continually increasing time.
- Keep increases below the dog's maximum time on the mat so that the dog doesn't get up before being rewarded and released.

## CROSS TRAINING OTHER BEHAVIORS

You could teach the dog to target a particular spot in your house such as the top of the stairs. Use this as a Place behavior when you answer the door. Sophia Yin (http://www.nerdbook.com/sophia/treat&train/) offers the Treat and Train™, a target training device and instructions to teach this behavior for dogs who are monsters when someone knocks on the door. This behavior could also be used for a Go Out in obedience or a table performance in agility.

## GO—THE DETAILS

1. Put the mat down, and mark and treat (or just treat) when the dog steps on the mat. If the dog remains on the mat, give a second, third or even fourth reward, then release the dog. Repeat 3-5 times. Note: From here on, we'll use the term "reward," meaning you can either mark and treat, or just give a treat to the dog, whatever your preference.

2. Reward for sitting on the mat. You can shape a sit, lure it with a treat if the dog doesn't know it well, or use a cue to get the dog to sit. Give the reward after the dog sits —he'll no longer get a treat just for getting on the mat. If he remains sitting, give a second, third or fourth reward, then release the dog. Repeat 3-5 times.

3. Reward the dog for lying down on the mat. You can shape, lure or cue it. Give the reward after the dog lies down. Give a second, third or fourth reward for remaining in the down, then release the dog. Repeat until the dog automatically lies down when he gets on the mat 8 of the 10 times (for two sessions) without waiting for a cue or a lure to lie down. Pick up your mat.

*Take a Break, Review Your Progress, Then Resume*

4. Now we are going to teach the dog to wait for a cue to go to the mat. Put your mat down, lightly hold on to the dog's collar, say your cue, then let go of the dog. The dog should immediately run to the mat

and lie down. (If not, go back to step 3 and work until the dog is correct 8 out of 10 times.) Give a second, third or fourth reward for remaining in the down, then release the dog. If you want to add an arm signal to your verbal cue, you can use a forward sweeping motion with your arm closest to the dog, or just point at the mat. From now on, you will only reward the dog if you have given your cue(s) first.

5.  You are now going to use your die to help you increase the amount of time the dog remains on the mat. Holding lightly onto the dog's collar, shake the die in your hand. Give your cue, let go of the dog, count the number of seconds the die indicated, then give a reward. Shake the die again, count the seconds, reward. Shake the die a third time, count the seconds, reward and release the dog off the mat. From now on, you will give from one to four rewards, waiting from one to six seconds between each reward (by using the die).

*8 correct? Move up a step (continue to use 8 correct for the remainder of the directions).*

6.  Continue as in step 5, but now double the second counts, either by rolling two dice or by just doubling one die. Continue gradually adding time, until the dog will remain on the mat for up to five minutes with only one reward. You will do this by bouncing around so that the amount of time between rewards and the number of rewards vary each time the dog is on the mat. In step 5, you averaged a reward every 3 seconds using 1 die, in step 6 the reward is on average every 6 seconds using 2 dice. Gradually increase your average time on the mat by continuing in the same manner.

*Take a Break, Review Your Progress, Then Resume*

7.  Gradually increase the distance to the mat. If you want to keep the mat in a particular place in your home, this is the time to train the dog to go to that spot. Remember that the distance should NOT increase incrementally, but sporadically. In other words, the dog has to go between 1-5 feet to the mat, averaging around 2.5 feet, but a different amount each time. Gradually increase the average until the dog is running from any place in the house to his mat, and remaining on it until released.

8. Add distractions—practice while you're cooking dinner, eating meals, while you're working with another dog, or while you answer the door for a package delivery. Think about how many different ways you could use this at home. To start adding distractions, make a list of 10 different levels of a distraction that you would have to train in order for the dog to be successful. For example, if you want to use this while you are eating dinner, the list might look like:

> On mat while you sit at table briefly, reward and release

> On mat while you pick up utensils and pretend to eat, reward and release.

> On mat while you take a few bites from a sandwich, reward and release.

> On mat while you eat most of a sandwich, reward and release.

> On mat while you set the table, then sit and eat a sandwich, reward and release.

> On mat while you set the table, returning to the kitchen for a "forgotten item", sit, eat, reward and release.

> And so on.

9. Take it out in public, to the park or a friend's house. Make a list of each of the places you want to practice in, and start with the least distracting and build up to the most distracting.

## HIP TOUCH

The dog will move his hip a short distance to touch a target and hold in place on the target until released. Our thanks to Gary Priest—Curator, Applied Behavior, Zoological Society of San Diego—for sharing his experience with teaching this to zoo animals such as elephants and walruses.

You'll work on confidence building for dogs who are afraid of having the rear end touched, and on generalizing touches to other body parts. You'll be learning how to shape against instinctive behavior, since the dog will most likely want to move away from the target rather than lean into it. You could shape the dog to target any other body part using the same method described below and a different target.

## GET READY

This type of behavior is commonly used with zoo animals in husbandry behaviors. Teaching the animal to offer a body part and hold still is very useful if you have to frequently test for some illness, and it gives the animal something to do while you clip nails or attend to other care needs. The beginning of the behavior (the side-step) can be used in Freestyle dance moves, or to teach the dog to bring his body closer to you for a start line in Agility, or to prepare for Heeling (a Finish) in Obedience. If your dog has learned a strong Spin or Turn, it may conflict with the early steps of this behavior.

An elephant targets the fence with her foot for cleaning and foot care.

Use a paddle (a ping pong paddle is perfect) or a flattish Frisbee™ or make a target by attaching a piece of cardboard cut in a circle to a dowel.

Target options for teaching touches with different body parts.

This behavior can be shaped with a verbal marker, but is best taught with a clicker because of the precision needed to get the hip bump and to quickly eliminate other target choices for the dog.

Before starting, you'll want to desensitize the dog to the hip target by touching the paddle or similar object against his hips and rear end, tapping him gently with it and moving it around him and marking and treating each time. Do this for at least 2 sessions of 10 treats each, or until the dog does not flinch or turn toward the target. This step is especially important if the dog is worried about objects touching his body, but will also help eliminate the target as a "nose" or "paw" touch option. Once the dog is comfortable with the touch of the target on his body, begin the training.

Should you train the dog to hit the target on both sides? It depends. It will be easier to train only one side, but if you decide later that you want the other side, you may have a challenge on your hands to shape it. Dogs (and humans!) tend to get "locked in" to their more comfortable side.

Since it can be confusing for a dog to be working both sides, you should consider whether you want the challenge at the beginning of the behavior, or be prepared to do it later, if you need to. There have been no studies to show which approach is better. In our opinion, you should incorporate both sides into the early stages of training so that both are options, and to keep the dog "balanced" physically. Consistently working only the dog's preferred side on behaviors can create a musculature difference from one side to the other.

## SUGGESTED CUES

"Place," "Butt," "Rump," "Bump."

## GO!

1.   Get the side-stepping behavior by using a treat at the dog's nose to pivot the dog's hip toward you (see photos below).

Getting the side step movement by pivoting in front of the dog. Notice the movement of the dog's right rear foot toward the trainer. This is what you will mark initially.

2.   Fade any food or hand motions as necessary.

3.     Build up to several side-steps. Be sure to work the dog on both sides.

4.     Hold the hip target next to the dog, about 1 inch away from her hip. Get the side-step, and mark and treat when your dog side-steps toward the target.

5.     Mark and treat when the dog touches the target.

6.     Gradually add distance, until the dog will move his hip into position from at least 6 inches away.

The target is held about 1" from the dog's hip to start with. Notice the movement of the dog's rear foot toward the handler, which brings the rear end towards the target.

7.     Increase duration until the dog will stay on the target up to 30 seconds.

8.     Add your cue.

9.     Vary where the target is held, staying approximately horizontal to the dog's hip but in different locations relative to the dog.

10.   You may also want to incorporate:

10a.  Movement variations—pivoting in a circle, or moving backward to the target.

These three photos show how to get a side-step movement by drawing a "U" pattern with a treat.

10b. Target variations—move to the target placed on chair, table or wall and remain there.

10c. Distractions—the dog keeps his hip in place even though you are doing something else with another part of his body (touching, brushing, etc), or if someone else is doing something with the dog.

## KEEP IN MIND

**Desensitize first.** If the dog seems sensitive to being touched on his rear, we recommend you spend several days getting him used to a touch with the target before starting the training. Start by creating a positive association to the target by putting the target where the dog can see it, and dropping several extra tasty treats on the floor. Pick up the target just before the dog finishes the treats. Continue until the dog seems happy to see the target, then gradually work it closer to the dog's rear end until you can gently touch him with it.

**The sides aren't the same.** You may find that the dog moves through the listed steps sooner on one side than the other. This is where having a helper or videotape for review can tell you what is going on. In Mandy's case, all three of her dogs were faster with this behavior on the left. A review of the videotape showed that she held her hand very differently when the dogs were on the right side. Her records also showed that the dogs made a lot more errors (touching with nose, biting at the target, or pawing at it) on the right side. During the training, one dog was touching the target with her hip on the left but was still working on a side-step, without a target, on the right side. You may have to "balance" your sessions, practicing more sessions on the weaker side until you get the dog touching the target. Make sure the dog meets your criteria for that step for that side, before upping your criteria.

## TROUBLESHOOTING

*Dog is frightened of the click or of being touched with the target.*
- Spend additional sessions getting the dog comfortable with the target and making it fun to get touched with it.
- Don't use the clicker, shape with a bridge word instead.
- Muffle the sound of the clicker so it isn't so sharp, or use an I-click™.

*Can't get the side-stepping motion.*
- Experiment with moving into the dog to see what makes them take a step to the side.
- Use barriers to allow movement only in the direction you want (remember to fade the barriers!)
- Teach the dog foot placement (see previous chapter) before trying this behavior.

*Dog keeps trying to touch the target with his nose or paw.*
- Work on the touching the target to the dog until the dog is not looking at or trying to touch the target with nose or paw.
- Keep track of the number of "wrong choices." Do not move to the next step unless the error rate is less than 2 out of 10 tries.

## CROSS TRAINING OTHER BEHAVIORS

Use the side-step (with or without a target) to build a cool dance step.

Teach the dog to touch his shoulder, neck, or ear to a target. It may help the dog discriminate to change the type of target for each body part. Teach the dog to move *away* from a target and *toward* a target, using different targets for each variation.

# GO—THE DETAILS

1. Use a treat held at the dog's nose to move the dog's hip in toward you. The dog may be facing you or beside you, and you will move the treat in the opposite direction of where you want the dog to step, or alternatively, in a U pattern drawn starting from in front of you, out, back and forward. Mark and treat each time the dog side-steps closer to you (see photos for help). Repeat one session (10 treats or one minute of work) on each side. It's easiest if you click the foot that is closest to you. Check the photos and experiment with your dog to determine the best hand and body movement to get the side-stepping with the rear feet.

2. Hold your hand as if you have a treat, and using the same motion in front of the dog's nose, mark and treat each time the dog moves a rear foot closer to you. Repeat one session (10 treats or one minute of work) on each side.

*Take a Break, Review Your Progress, Then Resume.*

3. Fade your hand signal by gradually making it less obvious. Continue to mark and treat a side-step toward you. Alternate sides each session.

4. Using just your body, step in front of the dog, mark and treat when the dog takes a step to the side, swinging her hip closer to you. Do one session (10 treats or one minute of work) on each side.

5. Add more steps until the dog is taking from one to five side-steps as you pivot around her in front.

*8 correct? Move up a step (and for the remainder of the directions).*

6. Hold the hip target next to the dog, about 1" away from her hip. Move in front of the dog to get the side-step, and mark and treat when your dog takes a step toward the target. The dog doesn't need to touch the target yet. Remember to work on each side in separate sessions.

7. Continue shaping until the dog is side-stepping into the target held about 1inch away, on both sides. When you are getting that consistently, you will mark the dog for actually touching the target, not just side-stepping.

8. Place the target an inch farther away from the dog and mark and treat when the dog touches. Try to anticipate when the dog is about to touch the target, so that your mark is properly timed with the actual touch rather than with the dog coming away from the target or stepping toward it.

9. Continue gradually adding distance, until the dog will move his hip into position from at least 6 inches away. Remember to vary the distance each time, so you are not just increasing every time, but bouncing between lots of easy, short movements and fewer longer ones. Work in short sessions of 10 treats, or up to one minute, each. Move to the next level when the dog is correct 8 out of 10 times.

*Take a Break, Review Your Progress, Then Resume.*

10. Increase duration until the dog will keep his hip on the target up to 30 seconds. Start by marking 1, 2, or 3 touches for a couple of sessions to get some variation in the length of touches. Now select out and mark and treat the longer touches. For more information on getting duration on a behavior, see Foot Touches in Chapter 3.

11. Add your cue. You will offer the target, then say your cue just before the dog does the behavior. Repeat 50-100 times over several sessions. You will no longer mark any touches without a verbal cue.

12. Vary where the target is held, staying approximately horizontal to the dog's hip but in different locations relative to the dog.

13. Depending on how you are going to use this behavior, you may want to incorporate:

    a. Movement variations—pivoting in a circle, or moving backward to the target.

    b. Target variations—moving to the target placed on chair, table or wall and remaining there.

    c. Distractions—the dog keeps his hip in place even though you are doing something else with another part of his body (touching, brushing, etc), or if someone else is doing something with the dog.

# 5
# "GOOD BEHAVIOR" TARGETS

Targets lend themselves to a variety of daily uses for the pet owner. Everybody wants a dog who will walk without pulling. Lots of people use head halters to help them control their dogs, but then have problems putting the halter on the dog. And certainly every dog owner needs the best "come when called" they can get! These behaviors are simple to get using a target, and easy for beginners to teach—either the dog touched the target or she didn't. All of the following behaviors are built from a nose touch.

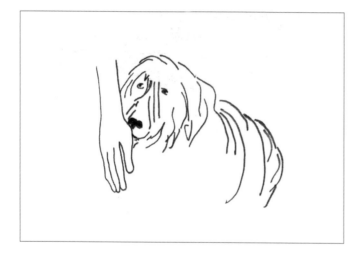

## GET DRESSED

We'll teach the dog to slip her head into a head collar (Halti™ or Gentle Leader™), regular collar, or fancy collar. For the head collar, we'll add a step to teach the dog to be comfortable having it on for a period of time.

This is a great behavior to work on confidence building in the dog and fading a target. If you teach it with a head collar, you'll also be working on duration.

## GET READY

If you teach the dog to put her head into a regular collar or fancy decorative collar you can put them on one handed—which makes this a practical behavior for a service dog. Plus, you'll impress your friends when you tell the dog to "get dressed!" If you have a dog who is worried about having things touch her head, this is a great way to work on overcoming that. You'll especially want to teach this if you walk your dog with a head collar, because it will help that go more smoothly.

Clockwise from left: Decorative collar, Halti™ (a head collar), Easy Walk Harness™

Before starting, you'll need to fit the dog for the appropriate size head collar if you choose to use one. But don't adjust the head collar to fit tightly on the dog just yet. It'll be easier to train the behavior and to get the dog comfortable with having it on for a period of time if it's loose initially. Once you have the dog comfortable wearing it, you can tighten it to the appropriate fit.

We'll build on the nose touch to your hand for this behavior, which means that both of your hands will be occupied. You may want to practice holding the collar, using your opposite hand as the target, then marking and delivering a treat a couple of times without the dog first.

## SUGGESTED CUES

"Dress," "Get Dressed," "Collar."

## GO!

1. Teach the Touch Nose to Hand in Chapter 2, up to adding the cue.
2. Hold the collar in one hand, and put the other hand into the opening. Mark and treat when the dog touches your hand.

The target hand is placed through the collar initially, then gradually closer to the center of the collar, and finally on the opposite side from the dog.

3. Move the hand slightly farther out of the collar opening, a few inches at a time.
4. If you're using a head collar, have the dog keep her head in the collar for a period of time by having her touch your hand multiple times.
5. Vary where you hold the collar so that the dog has to lift her head a bit, move her head down, or move it to one side or the other to get into the collar.
6. Add your cue.

7.   Fade your hand target.

8.   Have the dog step toward the collar to put her head in. Gradually add distance until the dog will take several steps to the collar to put her head in it.

9.   If you like, teach the dog to put her front feet on your shin or thigh to put her head in the collar.

10.   If you're using a head collar, gradually tighten it.

11.   Change rooms, work inside and outside on the behavior, so that the dog will do it regardless of where she is.

12.   Spend time working on the dog moving forward with a head collar on, then attaching a leash and walking with the leash on.

## KEEP IN MIND

**It's not just on and off.** The easiest way to work on duration (keeping her head in the head collar) is to just not mark the first time the dog touches. By this time, the dog will be expecting to get a treat, and will usually hit your hand again. Mark and treat the second touch. Continue to wait for one to three touches before marking and treating. Repeat several times, then remove the head collar. We don't want the dog to be trying to get the head collar off, and touching gives her something else to do.

## TROUBLESHOOTING

*Dog won't put her head through the collar.*

• Be careful not to put the collar *on* a sensitive dog—instead let her decide when to put her head *in* the collar and set the pace. You may have to back up a few steps and progress more slowly with your dog. Although it may take a bit longer, the payoff for you will be a dog who willingly puts her head into the collar.

## CROSS TRAINING OTHER BEHAVIORS

Can you teach the dog to back out of the training collar as well? Be sure you only do that with a dog that is safe off leash, just in case she decides to do it on her own. You'll want to make sure that behavior is solidly on cue.

# GO—THE DETAILS

1. Teach the dog to Touch Nose to Hand, as outlined in Chapter 2, up to the point that you add the cue.

2. Hold the collar (or head collar) in one hand, and put the other hand into the opening. Tell the dog to Touch, then mark and treat when the dog touches your hand. Repeat several times.

3. Move the hand slightly farther out of the collar opening. Cue the Touch, then mark and treat each time the dog touches your hand. Repeat several times. Continue moving gradually farther out, a few inches at a time, staying at each step for 5-10 treats, until the dog is putting her head eagerly through the collar.

4. If you're using a head collar, you'll need to train the dog to keep her head in the collar for a short period of time by having her touch multiple times before marking and treating.

*8 correct? Move up a step (and continue to use 8 out of 10 for the remaining steps).*

5. Vary where you hold the collar so that the dog has to lift her head a bit, move her head down, or move it to one side or the other to get into the collar. Remember to make your changes gradual enough that the dog can be successful.

6. Does the dog eagerly put her head through the opening regardless of where you put the collar? If so, you can add your "Dress" cue. To do this, tell the dog "Dress, Touch," then mark and treat the hand touch. Repeat 50-100 times, over the course of several sessions spread over a couple of days. Remember, don't mark any behavior that occurs without the cue from this point forward.

7. You'll no longer be marking the hand touch, but will instead be marking when the dog puts her head through the collar, so that you can gradually fade your hand out of the picture and drop the "Touch" cue.

8. Start about a step away from the dog and have the dog move toward the collar to put her head in. Continue to gradually add distance until the dog will take several steps to the collar to put her head in it, as many steps as you might need her to.

9. If you like, have the dog put her front feet on your shin or thigh to put her head in the collar. This is handy if you don't want to lean

down to the dog's level. Remember to start with a slight change from the straight on approach and gradually build up to the dog having to lift up to put her head into the collar. It may help to teach the dog separately, without the collar, to put her feet on your thigh.

10. If you're using a head collar, tighten it a teeny bit, then have the dog put her head into it, marking and treating after 1-10 seconds of having it on, varying the amount each time. Continue to gradually tighten the collar, moving as fast as you can with your individual dog.

11. Change rooms, work inside and outside on the behavior, so that the dog will do it regardless of where she is.

12. You'll need to spend some extra sessions working on the dog moving forward with a head collar on, then attaching a leash and walking with the leash on. Think about what you want to mark at each step (for example, is it forward movement or keeping the head still while the collar is on?)

# RECALL

We'll build on a nose touch to teach the dog to come to you from a distance. This is especially helpful if the dog is hard of hearing, because the hand signal is visible from a distance away.

## GET READY

The recall (Come) is, of course, an important basic skill for every dog. If you allow your dog off leash, you'll need to be able to call him from a distance, and the hand target lends itself well to that. We'll be building off Touch Nose to Hand from Chapter 2, so if you haven't taught that yet, work through those steps with your dog.

Before starting, make a list of at least 20 distractions for your dog and 10 different environments you could work in. Now list all the things your dog enjoys including treats, toys and activities. The more specific you are, the better.

In addition to your usual equipment, you'll need a long leash (30-50 feet) or confined areas to practice, until you feel confident having the dog "leash free." Keep in mind that some cities do not allow dogs off leash, or may restrict where they can be off leash. If you search, however, you may be able to find a local dog park for off leash play and practice. Use the dog park when there are no other dogs present in the initial stages, so that you can build on success with few distractions.

Not all dogs are safe or suited to being off leash. If your dog is not good with other dogs or with people, or has a tendency to chase small animals, you may need help from an experienced trainer.

## SUGGESTED CUES

"Dog's Name," "Come," "Here," "Touch"—all in combination with the hand signal (arm held out to side).

Using the Touch Nose to Hand for a recall signal.

## GO!

1.  Work to step 9 in Touch Nose to Hand in Chapter 2. Decide what you want to use as your cue and add it or change it as needed.

2.  Working in the lowest distraction environment, call your dog 3 or 4 times, timing each response, and figure out the average time it takes the dog to get to you to get a baseline time. Now using the hand touch and your verbal cue, mark and treat

responses that are *under* that time, and ignore any that are *over*.

3.  Increase distance, getting as far away as possible in that environment.

4.  Continue to add other environments until you have worked this in every room in the house.

5.  Wait until the dog is out of the room and cue the dog. Do several repetitions, varying the amount of time between each. Cue the touch from different rooms each time.

6.  Using your list of distractions, start with the lowest level distraction and cue the touch, mark and treat if the dog responds within the allotted time.

7.  Work through the same list of distractions, giving your cue when you are just out of sight of the dog. Remember to vary the time between repetitions.

8.  Change locations, building location distractions gradually. Vary the distance called on every repetition.

9.  Work on out of sight recalls outside.

## KEEP IN MIND

**N comes before O.** You can change to a new verbal cue by pairing it with the old cue. Say the new cue, then the old cue, then mark and treat when the dog does the behavior. It's easy to remember if you think of it alphabetically: N = new cue, then O = old cue.

**Cold trials.** "Cold trials" are the first response in any given work session or a single response that is separate from a work session. The dog hasn't had a chance to warm up by practicing yet. With this behavior, pay particular attention to the cold trials, as these are the ones we want to be under your baseline time. In real life, every time you'll need to get the dog back to you it will be a cold trial. Is the first response as fast and as intense as you'd like? If it's not, consider changing where you are working to make it easier, or giving the dog a rest.

**Multiply your rewards.** One way to use other types of rewards (besides treats) is to give the dog something higher on his list when he comes away from something low on the list. So coming away from a Nylabone™ gets you a new squeaky toy to play with for a short time. Another way to vary your rewards is the "double whammy"—he gives up something and gets a special treat or better reward, then gets to go back to what he gave up. So for example, he comes away from a person, gets a bit of steak, then gets to go back and greet the person again. Real life often looks like this. If the dog is willingly coming away from whatever he is doing, you know you have ordered your list of rewards and distractions correctly!

# TROUBLESHOOTING

*Dog won't touch hand.*

- Review Troubleshooting in Touch Hand to Nose for problem-solving tips.

*Dog comes slowly.*

- Don't do too many repetitions in a session—it's better to spread the sessions out.
- Work before meals, using tasty treats.
- Work in a location with fewer distractions.
- If this is the case only in certain rooms, it may be that the dog has unpleasant associations with that room (such as bath time, going into a kennel, or getting his toenails clipped). You may have to work just outside the room initially.

*Dog doesn't come when out of sight, or with distractions.*

- Make sure the response to your verbal cue is strong, by saying it just before you present your hand. If you do this 50-100 times over several training sessions, the dog will start to respond on the verbal cue. Many dogs rely primarily on the hand signal.
- Go back and build up distractions more slowly. You will need to have many distractions levels between "leaves blowing around" and "squirrels playing," for example.
- Distance is one way to decrease your distractions—try moving farther away and see if the response is better.

# CROSS TRAINING OTHER BEHAVIORS

See if you can get your "hand-touching-fool" of a dog to touch your hand when it's hidden behind your back or otherwise difficult to touch, so that he learns to really search for the target (your hand).

Do a back-and-forth hand touch with another person, or several other people. The dog has to learn to respond to the person that gives the cues.

## GO—THE DETAILS

1. Work to step 9 in Touch Nose to Hand in Chapter 2. You'll need to decide at this point what you want to use as your cue(s). We recommend you use a verbal cue (a command) in addition to the visual cue of your arm being held out. If you want to change your hand touch cue to a new verbal cue for the recall, do that first (see Keep in Mind above). But you don't have to change the cue, and if the dog has a so-so response to Come or his name, it might be to your advantage to stick with the current cue for Touch Nose to Hand if the touch response is strong.

2. We want the dog to come quickly, so we are going to build that in at the outset. Working in your lowest distraction environment (for most people that's the kitchen!) call your dog and time how long it takes for him to get to you from the other side of the room. Repeat 3 or 4 times and figure out the average. This is your baseline time. You will only mark responses that are *under* that time, and ignore any that are *over*. All cold trials (the first recall in each work session) should be under the baseline before moving to the next step.

*8 correct? Move up a step.*

3. Increase distance gradually, getting as far away as possible in that location, bouncing around the distance so that you aren't always getting farther away. In other words, many times the dog is close, and only once in a while is he far away. We want lots of easy-to-succeed opportunities in the early stages. We are marking and treating the dog each time for a touch within the allotted time at this step.

4. Change to another room (with slightly more distractions) and repeat the last step. Continue to add other locations until you have worked this in every room in the house. Remember that the dog is only marked and treated if he touches your hand in the allotted time.

5. Now we'll focus on cold trials. Wait until the dog is out of the room (you can have someone hold him or just take advantage of him being elsewhere). The dog must touch your hand in the allotted time or he doesn't get marked and treated. Do one repetition, then try another

several minutes later (try to vary the amount of time between repetitions). Call from different rooms each time. Understand that at this point the dog is responding only to the verbal cue, but don't worry, it is probably pretty strong. If not, see Troubleshooting for some tips. If you are working with a deaf dog, a hard stomp on the floor can help to get their attention and be used instead of a verbal cue. Another option is to use a vibrating collar as your recall cue combined with a hand touch. See www.deafdogs.org for more information on working with deaf dogs and sources for a vibrating collar.

6. Using your list of distractions, start with the lowest level distraction and call the dog away from it. For example, maybe chewing on a Nylabone™ is at the bottom of your dog's list of favorite things to do. Next time he is chewing on the bone, stand in front of him and cue the touch, mark and treat if he responds within the allotted time. Continue to progress through your distractions as long as the dog is responding well with each distraction. If he doesn't respond, you need something lower on your distraction list!

7. Work through the same list of distractions in a new location. Remember to vary the time between repetitions, and only mark and treat responses that are under the required time. You'll also want to occasionally call the dog away from a distraction when you are out of sight.

8. Change locations again, building up to more distracting locations gradually. Vary the distance from very close to the maximum you might need on every repetition. Remember that bouncing around is most effective if there are many "easy" distances and only occasional "hard" or "very hard" choices.

9. Once you get outside, decide if you want to work on out of sight recalls. It's worth practicing, but does require that the dog not be visible to you for short periods. One way around this is to have someone else observe the dog while you're working, so he doesn't get into trouble, and to work in a confined area. Intersperse occasional out of sight calls with frequent easier ones.

# HEEL OFF LEASH

The dog will walk next to you while off leash, head even with your pant leg, and stop when you stop. Using a target allows you to position the dog's nose (and therefore body) exactly where you need it.

We'll work on following a target, as well as duration in another form—distance or number of steps covered.

## GET READY

This behavior can also be taught without a target, but using a target is much easier for beginner dogs and students, as it gives a specific behavior to mark and reward.

The instructions here are for the pet rather than competition dog. You can get more precision by placing the target exactly where you want the dog's nose to be, for example using a bit of tape on your pants seam or a target stick held slightly ahead of your left leg.

You'll build on the Touch Nose to Hand or Target Stick for this behavior. If you have a smaller dog or have difficulty bending over to use a hand target, use the target stick instead. Before working with the dog, practice walking (holding your hand out or using the target stick), marking (clicking or using a bridge word) and handing a treat to your pretend dog *beside* you (and not in front) until you can do it smoothly while in motion.

If you are planning to compete in Obedience, you'll want to discuss with your instructor exactly where the dog needs to have her head for good heeling position. Figure out where your target needs to be in order to get the head in the correct position.

## SUGGESTED CUES

"Touch," "Heel," "Trot," "Stride."

## GO!

1. Working on either the Touch Nose to Hand or Target Stick behavior from Chapter 2, progress until the dog will follow a moving target.

2. Sit the dog or have her stand next to you at your side. Take one step forward, telling the dog Touch as you move forward. Mark and treat when the dog touches.

Placement for a hand target used in heeling.

3.    Gradually add more steps until the dog is moving forward up to 30 steps with one treat. Mark and treat touches.

4.    Mark and treat based on number of steps now instead of touching, working up to 30 steps.

5.    Change your cue to your heeling cue.

6.    Gradually fade the target, over a period of several sessions.

7.    Work in gradually more distracting environments.

## TROUBLESHOOTING

*Dog is okay in low level distractions (house) but behavior falls apart in the real world.*

• Work Heel On Leash first. See next section.

• Work in a confined area so you feel confident that the dog won't take off and you can wait for the behavior you will mark and treat.

• Use more "in-between" locations (see Chapter 2 for suggestions on how to break down practice locations).

*Behavior disappears when target disappears.*

- Go back to step 4, making sure you are marking *before* the dog touches. Have someone watch you, or review your videotape, to see if you are marking at the right time.
- Reintroduce the target and fade it more slowly, adding at least one step in between each of your original steps in the fading process.

## CROSS TRAINING OTHER BEHAVIORS

Add some fancy turns and figure 8s through your legs to build a dance sequence for you and your dog. Set it to music and you can wow your friends and family with how clever you and your dog are.

Using a piece of tape placed on your pant leg or elbow, or a target stick, work on more precise heeling for competition level performance. You'll need to fade the target rather quickly since you don't want the dog bumping your pant leg in competition, as well as add sits and work on turns and changes of speed. Add the fast sits, turns and change of speed separately and chain it into the heeling.

## GO—THE DETAILS

1. Working on the Touch Nose to Hand or Target Stick, progress until the dog will follow a moving hand or target stick (from here on we'll refer to both as the target) independently of you.

2. Sit the dog or have her stand next to you at your side (left side is required for obedience competition, but you can teach the right if that's more comfortable for you and you're not competing). Experiment without the dog to see which side works better for you. Let your hand hang naturally at your side. If you are using the target stick, hold it in the hand closest to the dog (left hand) so that the tip will be right where you want the dog's nose. Take one step forward, telling the dog Touch as you move forward. Mark and treat when the dog touches. Try to deliver the treat exactly where you want the dog to be instead of in front of you. Put the dog next to you again and repeat until the dog is eagerly moving forward when you say Touch. Remember not to reward any touches without the verbal cue, instead just reset the dog.

*8 correct? Move up a step (and continue to use 8 out of 10 for the remaining steps).*

3. Gradually add more steps. You'll do this by bouncing around between one and three steps to start with. Decide before you move forward how many steps the dog must go to touch the target for that repetition. When the dog is successful 8 out of 10 times for two sessions in a row, add another step so that you are varying between one and four steps. (Remember that you want many more one and two step touches and fewer three and four step touches). Continue adding steps, until the dog will take between 1 and 30 steps forward in a straight line with only one mark and treat.

4. Now we are going to mark *just before* the dog touches the target. Instead of touching, we are marking the dog for a pre-determined number of steps. Do several sessions of this, until the dog is following, but not touching, the target up to 30 steps in a straight line.

5. If you wish to change your cue (the dog is no longer touching, so it would be appropriate to give this a different name), do it now. The process is Heel (new cue), Touch (old cue), mark and treat for the dog stepping forward the required number of steps. You can drop the old cue when the dog is moving forward on Heel.

6. Gradually fade the target, over a period of several sessions, by making it smaller or less visible each session. So if you are using a hand touch, you will pull it up to your waist gradually. For a target stick, hold it closer and closer to the end until just the tip is showing.

7. Work in gradually more distracting locations.

## TROUBLESHOOTING FOR COMPETITORS

Following are some special notes for competitors. These tend to be the biggest problem areas. We recommend you use a clicker as your marker, as the precision will be helpful to problem-solving.

**Lagging—the dog walks slightly behind you.**
Start walking slowly in a large circle clockwise. Click every time the dog is in the correct spot, but deliver the treat about one foot in front of the dog's nose. As you practice this, the dog should start to anticipate that the treat will be a little forward and move up closer to your leg. It may also help to start this with a target held slightly in front of where you want the dog to be.

On a straight line, toss the reward in front of the dog. If you use food as a reward, toss it in such a manner so he doesn't have to spend a long time searching for it. Start with one step, click, toss the toy or treat. Gradually add more steps.

Start walking in a square pattern clockwise (following the pattern on large cement squares will help keep you straight, or draw a large square on the ground with chalk). Each time you turn to the right, click and treat the dog for being in correct position at your side. Your instructor can show you the proper footwork for a right turn, to help the dog anticipate it. Deliver your reward about one foot in front of the dog each time after clicking. Move from a square pattern to an about turn as the dog starts to get it.

**Forging—the dog is consistently ahead of you.**
Work in counterclockwise circles, clicking the correct position and delivering the reward slightly *behind* the dog's head.

In straight lines, deliver the treat behind the dog slightly.

Use a square pattern counterclockwise to work on the dog moving out of your way as you turn. Deliver your rewards slightly behind the dog. Again, talk to your instructor about the proper footwork for this turn. You might also review the notes in Chapter 4 for teaching the dog to move his hip to a target to get a nice swing into position as you turn. Progress to a left about turn as the dog gets better.

**Fast sits in heel position on stopping.**
Time how long it takes the dog to sit when you stop. Take the average of three of the sits and use that as your maximum—meaning that the dog only gets clicked and treated if he sits within the allotted time. Take one step forward, and click and treat if the dog sits fast enough. When the dog is successful 8 out of 10 times for two sessions in a row, decrease the allotted time gradually. Continue until the sits are as fast as you like. Now add more steps, varying how many steps you take before you stop. Deliver all of your rewards in place, slightly above the dog's head to keep the head up. For some dogs, throwing the reward may also speed up the sit. That will also help with dogs who are sluggish getting up from a sit to start heeling again.

**Distractions.**
Working in a low distraction area that is secure (or with the dog on a long leash) start moving forward in a large counterclockwise circle, ignoring the

dog. When the dog comes to your side, click and deliver the treat beside you. Don't stop walking. Gradually build up the number of steps the dog has to take beside you before you click and treat. When the dog is beside you taking several steps at a time, move to a new, more distracting, location. Continue adding more distracting locations as the dog gets better. Repeat the entire process walking in a clockwise circle (this direction is a bit harder for the dog to remain in the correct position).

# HEEL ON LEASH

The dog will walk next to you while on leash, maintaining position with his head even with your leg, and stop and sit when you stop.

## GET READY

Here we'll use the leash as a target for the dog. Using a leash will make the positioning less precise than needed for competition so this variation is more appropriate for pet owners. Competitors can use a target on their pant leg instead, following the directions for Heel Off Leash, to get the accuracy necessary for competition.

It doesn't matter whether you teach this or the Heel Off Leash first. We gave directions for the off leash work first because it is actually easier to work without having to worry about a leash.

The basic steps to get the behavior are pretty straightforward now that you've practiced so many different types of nose touches with your dog. Where the behavior gets challenging is in taking it "on the road"—out into the real world where there are other dogs, people, smells and critters to distract your dog. To this end, we'll offer up some suggestions for using a variety of rewards found in real life, and give some suggestions for how to make on leash greetings with other dogs go smoothly. We recommend that you use the heel position for crossing streets, passing people and dogs, and navigating crowds, and have a looser criteria (such as no pulling on leash) for the majority of your walk. Trying to maintain a heel for the entire walk would be exhausting for both you and the dog.

You'll need a comfortable 4-6 foot leash in addition to your usual equipment for this behavior. The list of distractions and working locations you created for the Heel Off Leash will also come in handy. The clicker is useful to teach this, however, you may find it a challenge to hold on to the clicker, leash and dog and deliver treats. If so, feel free to use a bridge word instead. Before getting your dog, practice holding on to everything, marking and delivering treats to your left side *while in motion*. When you can do that comfortably, go and get your dog.

## SUGGESTED CUES

"Heel," "Trot," "Let's Go," or just the presence of the leash.

You can use the same cue you used for Heel Off Leash. If you are planning on competing, you might want to have a different cue for loose leash walking (the kind you do daily) vs. the precise heeling required for the ring.

## GO!

1.      Clip your leash to a piece of furniture, so that it is horizontal. Mark and treat when the dog touches it anywhere.
2.      Gradually make the leash more vertical until it is completely vertical.

Starting position for leash target. The leash is almost horizontal.

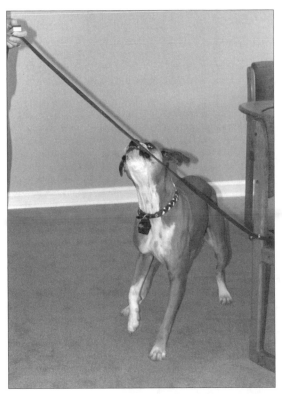

Gradually make the leash more vertical.

3.  Position the leash next to your leg and work on the touches.
4.  Attach the leash to the dog and repeat the last step.
5.  Get the dog touching multiple times.
6.  Take one step and have the dog touch one, two or three times. Add more steps as the dog is successful, varying the number of steps until the dog is taking 5 to 10 steps forward to touch.
7.  Have the dog touch while you're still in motion and deliver the treat while you are still moving forward.
8.  Change locations until you have worked in at least 5 different places.
9.  Add more steps in between treats, stopping after each treat. Remember not every touch gets marked and treated.
10.  Add the Sit behavior by cuing the dog to Sit as you stop.
11.  Continue until the dog is starting to anticipate the Sit. Alternate how often you feed the Sit.
12.  Add a heel cue, if you wish.
13.  Take it on the road to different locations.

14. Vary your rewards by using the opportunity to greet another dog or a person, or to go and sniff, instead of treats.

15. Now vary how many times the dog has to touch, or sit, before marking and releasing the dog for his reward. Call him back each time for a treat.

The dog is now following the leash rather than touching it.

## KEEP IN MIND

**Randomize yourself.** It's tough for humans to be random—they easily fall into patterns. Whenever the instructions call for a varied number of touches or steps, you might want to write down a random number for each of 10 repetitions. Then read the next number from your list, or have someone call out the next number for you.

## TROUBLESHOOTING

*The dog has difficulty touching the leash, or seems to lose the behavior, once the leash is vertical.*

• Go back and put more steps in between your original steps.

*You can't get any heeling at all in public.*
- Make your transition to more distracting locations more gradual.
- Practice greetings in the least distracting locations first.
- Move farther away from a distraction, until you get the behavior, then release the dog to sniff or greet.
- Increase your rewards.
- Shorten your work sessions.
- If you're really having difficulty, you might want to fit the dog with a head collar or walking harness (Easy Walk™) to prevent pulling on walks.

# CROSS TRAINING OTHER BEHAVIORS

How fast can you get the dog to sit when you stop? Can you fool the dog by slowing down or almost stopping (a great way to "proof" for competition heeling). Add right and left turns, fast and slow to the on leash heel behavior.

## GO—THE DETAILS

1. Clip your leash to a piece of furniture, so that it is horizontal, parallel to the ground. Mark and treat when the dog first looks at it, then sniffs, then touches it. Don't stay too long at each of these steps – only 4-5 repetitions. It should go very quickly once the dog realizes he should touch it with his nose rather than some other body part. We don't want the dog to try and touch the end of the leash, so anywhere on the leash counts.
2. Gradually make the leash more vertical by clipping it to an object closer to the floor. Work as quickly as you can to get the leash completely vertical.

*8 correct? Move up a step. (Continue to use 8 out of 10 correct throughout.)*

3. Position the leash next to your leg but not attached to the dog. Mark and treat when the dog touches.
4. Attach the leash to the dog and repeat the last step. The leash will need to be held a little bit in front of the dog's nose for him to comfortably touch it.
5. Get the dog touching multiple times by not marking the first touch. Instead, mark and treat when the dog touches one, two or three times.

Vary how many touches you require each time—see Keep in Mind for tips.

6. With the leash on the dog, take one step and have the dog touch one, two or three times. Add more steps as the dog is successful, varying the number of steps by bouncing around a gradually increasing average. When the dog will take between 5 and 10 steps forward consistently, without getting distracted, before getting a treat, go on to the next step.

7. Have the dog touch the leash while you're still in motion. So the dog will now be following the leash moving ahead of him, trying to touch it. Mark and treat after 5 to 10 steps, delivering the treat while you are still moving forward. At the end of 10 repetitions, the dog will have taken at least 50-100 steps with no stopping, with only 10 treats, so you need to plan space for this. You don't need to reward every leash touch, but make sure you reward often enough that the dog wants to continue playing the game.

8. Change locations, working in a bit more distracting area, and repeat the previous step. Continue changing locations until you have worked in at least 5 different places.

9. Now add more steps in between treats, but instead of continuing, stop after you give each treat. Because not every touch is rewarded, you will only be stopping after you give a treat. Sometimes the dog will touch the leash and you will continue more steps ahead. On average though, the dog needs to be rewarded every 30 to 50 steps. Don't make the rewards too rare, or the dog may stop playing this game with you.

10. Add the Sit behavior by cuing the dog to Sit as you stop. So a pattern might look like this: Both moving 9 steps forward, touch leash, 5 steps forward, touch leash/mark/treat, stop, cue Sit, reward Sit, repeat (for a different number of steps). Remember it may help to write out a plan with at least 10 treats given.

11. Continue until the dog is starting to anticipate the Sit when you stop, and doing it automatically before you cue the Sit. Now alternate how often you feed the Sit. So as you start to stretch out the rewards, some-times the dog will get treats for sitting, and sometimes for touching the leash. A common mistake that people make is to only reward the Sit. We want the dog to stay beside us, so the leash touch must also be rewarded.

12. Add your Heel cue, if you wish. You will say your cue just before you step forward. If you choose not to have a verbal cue, the leash provides a strong visual cue.

13. Take it on the road to different locations. You may have to give more frequent rewards in more distracting locations, especially the first few times in a new place.

14. You can vary your rewards, by using the opportunity to greet another dog, greet a person, or to go and sniff, instead of treats. Choose the least distracting of those three options for your dog for your initial training sessions, then work the second most distracting, and so on. As an example, we'll use the opportunity to sniff as the least distracting. Find something smelly that your dog likes, such as a bush or fence corner. Start about 10 feet away from the spot, and start walking toward it. When the dog touches the leash, mark and release the dog to sniff. Call the dog back and reward with a treat. Repeat the process several times, coming at the distraction from different directions and starting at varying distances away   Continue to practice with a variety of real life distractions while on walks. You may be able to completely wean the dog off of treats by using the opportunity to investigate as a reward, or you may need the occasional tasty goodie to entice him away from a particularly good distraction. But most dogs are better behaved if they are frequently allowed to explore than if they are restricted from it completely.  You can vary what you require from the dog (touch the leash or sit), what he gets to do (sniff or greet) and his reward when he comes back to you to keep it interesting.  We also recommend you keep greetings short to prevent the dog from getting overly excited.  Instead, repeat the greeting several times for a few seconds each time.

15. Now vary how many times the dog has to touch, or sit, before marking and releasing the dog for his reward. Call him back each time for a treat.

# 6

# TARGETS FOR AGILITY

In this chapter, you'll learn how to use targets to help you in agility competition. But before you get started, we have a couple of homework assignments for you. Discuss with your agility instructor the cues you'll use for obstacles. List them out, as well as common cue words you use such as your release word, the dog's name, and basic behaviors. Make a list and define each of them so that you are clear there are no conflicts or muddied cues (or too many cues that start with "T"!). We recommend that you pick cues that are short and easy to remember, as you'll be saying them quickly while you're running a course. Traditionally, a different cue is used for each of the contact obstacles, open and closed tunnels, and sometimes for spread jumps versus regular jumps. But consider whether you'll really need all those different cues (and use them while running) with your own dog.

Your second homework assignment is to read the rules for any organization you want to compete in, so that you are familiar with jump heights, how contact equipment is judged, and other regulations. You can find them on line at: www.usdaa.com, www.nadac.com, www.k9cpe.com, www.akc.org, www.ukcdogs.com. Mixed breed dogs can compete in all except AKC.

We'll use the nose touch behavior in several ways, make use of a foot target, and transfer a body target. In some cases, you'll need to have the actual equipment or a reasonable facsimile to progress, but we'll give you tips on using stuff you already may have available around the house for the initial stages of training.

Remember that we will be abbreviating the instructions for these behaviors, and you will need to "fill in the blanks"—steps in between the ones we've listed. If you run into difficulties, it will be helpful for you to take a break, review your training notes and/or video, and see if you need to add even more shaping steps to your plan. In most cases, adding shaping steps will fix the problem. Also note that these instructions are just one way to get to the end behavior. You might come up with a better way if you brainstorm for a bit. For some behaviors, the basic instructions are straightforward so we won't bother with a separate, more detailed set of instructions. If you have difficulty, go back and review the first four chapters or ask a friend to help you problem solve.

This chapter does presume that you are working with an agility instructor or knowledgeable friend, or that you have some experience in competing, as we will only give you the jumping-off point for these behaviors, not the finished product. You'll have to know how to incorporate them into working on agility equipment, or know when they'll be useful.

 # FRONT AND REAR CROSSES

Building on Touch Nose to Hand, you will teach your dog to turn into you and away from you by following your body language. You can build on this to use as a front or rear cross in competition.

## GET READY

As you run an agility course with your dog, you'll need to be able to change sides to get from obstacle to obstacle in the best way. This is called a "cross." These are basic handling maneuvers that you'll use again and again, so it will be very beneficial for you and your dog to get comfortable and smooth with them. Plus the hand touching behavior is a great warm up for your dog while you're waiting to go into the ring, allowing for frequent rewards with a fairly simple, snappy behavior.

During this training the dog is learning to pay attention to your shoulder, body and hands. This may cause you some problems if you compete in other areas such as obedience, especially if the dog takes the turn quickly, with a minimum of movement from you, or if you have a tendency to be sloppy with your signals.

Practice your mechanics first! Have a friend pretend to be your dog until you are smooth, understand exactly where you will mark the behavior and deliver the treat, and how it should look. You can teach both crosses at the same time, as your dog will be relying on your body language to tell him which direction to go. The marking point of the turn is the same for both although your body language will look different to the dog for each. Remember to work only one type of cross in a session, and to work in short sessions of 3-5 minutes maximum. Set a timer if you need to!

You can teach this readily using a verbal marker. No special equipment is required to teach it, but you'll want to add jumps and tunnels to these crosses as you build on this skill with the dog. Here's a behavior that's so quick and easy, we won't even ask you to record anything.

## SUGGESTED CUES

Body/shoulder/arm cues (built into the training), "Turn," "Left"/"Right."

# GO!

1.  Complete all the steps in Chapter 2 on the Touch Nose to Hand behavior.
2.  Take one step away from the dog, put out your hand, say Touch, and let the dog move forward to touch the hand. Mark and treat when he touches. Move on to the next step when the dog is successful 8 out of 10 times.
3.  Repeat this step with the other hand. For each remaining step, work one session with the right hand, and one session with the left hand.

*8 correct? Move up a step. (Continue to use 8 correct throughout instructions.)*

4.  Take between one to three steps away, tell the dog to Touch, mark and treat when he touches. Vary the number of steps each time.
5.  Take one step away, tell the dog to Touch, then as the dog moves to touch, take another step, so that you are both moving forward at the same time. Mark and treat when the dog touches. Continue at this step until the dog will *follow* your hand (both of you moving forward) for up to 5 steps. Remember that you will need to plan out how to get from one step to five steps, "bouncing around" as you go.
6.  Now we will change our criteria from touching the hand to moving forward. The dog is now marked and treated for taking steps rather than for the touch. Continue to build steps with the dog following your hand. Work up to 10 steps where the dog will follow your hand, making sure to vary the number of steps each time. (You no longer need to tell the dog to "Touch".)
7.  Start moving forward a couple of steps, then execute your turn. Mark when the dog initiates the turn, and treat as he comes out of the turn:

a. Front cross:  Make a U turn toward the dog, changing hands as the dog turns *toward* you. The dog and you will both turn in place, so you both reverse directions and the dog ends up following the opposite hand. The shoulder closest to the dog at the start of the turn (called the inside shoulder) drops and reverses direction to indicate the turn, if you do this correctly.

b. Rear cross: Make a U turn toward the dog, using the arm and hand closest to the dog to get the dog to start the turn *away* from you, then have the dog follow your opposite hand when you both turn. The hand closest to the dog at the start of the turn goes slightly up and forward to indicate the turn. It may help you to think of dog being "thrown away" from you with first hand and "caught" with the other.

This is where you should mark the front cross (the dog is starting the turn)…

Then deliver the treat slightly out of the turn.

This is where the rear cross should be marked (as the dog starts the turn)…

Then deliver the treat slightly past the turn.

The Front Cross

The Rear Cross

8.    Repeat with the dog starting on your opposite side.

9.    Continue practicing both crosses, on both sides of your body, until the dog is initiating the turn as soon as you start to change direction. This is a helpful spot to have an observer watch you and say out loud which cross she thinks you will be making as soon as she recognizes it.

10.   Add a verbal cue for the cross if you wish at this point.

11.    Increase the dog's speed out of the turn by using a toy thrown as a reward rather than a treat. You may need to teach the dog to be interested in toys to do this step. For more information, see Get Ready in the Go On behavior later in this chapter. The turn is marked when the dog starts it, and the toy is thrown on completion of the turn, forward in the direction you are facing after turning, using the arm closest to the dog. So if the turn is started with the dog on your left, the toy will be thrown with the right arm.

12.    Increase your speed gradually, until you can do these crosses with your dog while at a fast walk, jogging, and then at a run.

13.    Work in different locations to generalize the behavior. This is an easy behavior to take to different parks for practice. No schlepping equipment!

## TROUBLESHOOTING

*Dog not turning in correct direction.*

- Have a friend pretend to be your dog, responding to the direction they think you're going.
- Use a treat lure to get the turn—hold treats in each hand, start the dog with one hand, "catch" with the other and reward.
- Mark at a slightly later point in the turn, when you are sure the dog will complete it correctly.

## CROSS TRAINING OTHER BEHAVIORS

Incorporate obstacles before or after the cross (figure 8s or jumps, etc.), starting with easy obstacles and adding more difficult ones (contacts, etc) as you and the dog become more fluid.

 ## GO ON

The dog will run a distance away from you (20 to 30 feet) in a straight line in the direction she's facing, taking any obstacles in her path, to touch a contact disk on the ground with her nose. We will fade (get rid of) the contact disk, so that the dog will run straight until told to do something else. In agility, you will also use an "Out" where the dog moves laterally away from you in a straight line (see photos for the difference in dog's directional movement and your arm signal).

This behavior works on adding distance and speed to a target, and chaining cues. We'll also talk about how to use rewards effectively to keep the dog from turning back to you.

# GET READY

This is a core behavior you'll need for competition, particularly if you are not a fast runner! You will often be behind the dog on a straight line of jumps or may want to cut corners so you don't have to run as much.

We want to get the dog running directly to the target in the early stages rather than searching for it, so it's helpful to build distance slowly and work on pavement at first so the target is easy for the dog to see.

If the dog is keen on toys or balls, these are excellent rewards to use because they encourage movement (chasing), unlike treats, which encourage standing and eating. If your dog isn't very interested in toys, you can buy a variety of toys with Velcro™ closures that allow them to be stuffed with treats. Spend some time teaching the dog to tug the toy and getting clicked and treated for it. If you need assistance with this behavior, see Tug in Chapter 7, or check out Susan Garrett's *Ruff Love*, an excellent book on motivating your dog, or purchase a Tug-N-Treat™ from www.cleanrun.com and use the directions included on the website. If you plan on competing in agility, you'll need a dog who is interested in a variety of rewards (toys, treats, chasing you, playing with you) to compete effectively, so get to it and build this skill!

Before you go get your dog, practice delivering your reward accurately on or ahead of the target. This helps teach the dog it's good to work away from you, a difficult skill for a green dog. If all rewards come from you, the dog will want to be close to you. Put your target out approximately 5 feet away, mark and toss the treat or toy on the target or slightly ahead (away from where you are standing). Continue adding distance until you can do this smoothly up to 30 feet away from the target.

Set a "time standard" before moving on to each step by having a friend hold your dog while you run away to the distance you'll be working at, teasing with a toy. Let the dog go and time how long it takes her to run to you. This is a reasonable speed to complete one repetition of the behavior. Add a few seconds to allow for the training situation. This time standard will tell you whether the dog is having difficulty, needs a break or whether you need to re-evaluate your

Some options for make-at-home equipment, clockwise from left: PVC jumps, wobble board, PVC on soda cans, rain gutter.

criteria for that step. Continue as long as the dog is working within the time allotted for that step.

You'll need all your usual equipment as well as a clicker, contact disk, and eventually a set of jumps. The advantage of a clicker as a marker over a bridge word is that the dog is less likely to turn back to you.

If you don't have jumps, you can rig a reasonable substitute by using 4 to 5 foot lengths of 1/2 inch PVC set on crushed soda cans or cement blocks. However, if you are considering competition, it would be a good idea to invest in a set of four PVC jumps and maybe a tunnel or two. Check out eBay for portable options (type in "agility jumps" or "portable jumps"). If you're handy, you can make your own PVC jumps.

Remember to keep your work sessions very short as the dog will be expending a lot of energy, especially once jumps are added. We recommend no more than three minutes per session, and three to five sessions per day. Set a timer if you have a tendency to go longer than that. With all agility behaviors, speed and accuracy are of primary importance. It will do you no good in the long run to train the dog to fatigue. Instead, work with a fresh dog and quit while she's still begging to work!

## SUGGESTED CUES

"Go," "Go On."

# GO!

1. Complete all the steps in the Contact Disk behavior in Chapter 2.
2. Vary your location every session, gradually working up to being outside on pavement.
3. Gradually add distance, until the dog will run up to 30 feet away from you to the target, without veering off path or searching for the target.

The arm signal for "Go On"

The arm signal for "Out"

4. Add the Go cue. You will chain this cue with the Contact cue in the order "Go"— "Contact," then mark and treat when the dog touches the target.

5. Work other locations that are not on pavement, decreasing the distance to five feet and gradually building up to 30 feet.

6. Set the target at least 35 feet away. Give your Go cue, but mark the dog before he gets to the target, then toss the toy ahead of the dog.

7. Add equipment, starting with jumps.

8. Start moving behind the dog, first walking, then jogging, and then running.

9. Practice in a variety of locations, with a variety of equipment.

## KEEP IN MIND

**Anticipation works in your favor.** Pairing "Go" and "Contact" together makes the dog anticipate that when you say "Go," "Contact" will be next. This works to your advantage when you want to drop the Contact cue. If the dog will not move away from you without the additional Contact cue, you can continue to use it paired with Go. It is a bit sloppy if you are not going to allow the dog to touch the target, but it's not a big deal. However, you'll want to drop the Contact cue as soon as you are able to.

## TROUBLESHOOTING

*Dog is slow going to touch contact.*
- Make sure the dog is fresh
- Decrease your distance until you get the level of speed you want.
- Increase your reward level
- Work just before meals
- Reduce or eliminate all distractions
- Train for speed by only clicking touches that are within your allotted time. Gradually decrease the time allowed for the "run to touch" behavior.

*Dog refuses to go over jumps, or is very slow over jumps.*
- Get the dog used to jumps as a separate step (ask for help from your instructor).
- Have dog checked by a vet for physical limitations or injuries (a very real and common possibility).
- Reduce the dog's weight.

*Dog searches for contact, or looks for the treat after touching contact.*
- Decrease distance until the dog is going directly to contact. Gradually increase again.
- Increase the size of the contact, or use an opaque contact (note that it will be harder to fade these).
- Use a thrown toy or treats in a container as a reward.

*Dog turns back to you after being marked.*
- Have someone check or videotape to ensure that you are marking the dog while she is moving/looking forward and then delivering the reward smoothly in front of her before she has a chance to look back
- Practice with a tunnel as your first obstacle, mark while the dog is in the tunnel and throw the toy *before* the dog exits the tunnel. After several sessions of this, the dog should actually pick up speed upon hearing the marker, expecting his reward to be in front of him.

# CROSS TRAINING OTHER BEHAVIORS

How fast and how far can you get the dog to go in a straight line?

Teach the dog to take a number of jumps, then turn away from the next one when cued (Hint: You'll need your crosses from the last section for this one!)

The directions are similar for teaching a Go Out for Utility in Obedience, where the dog runs in a straight line until told to Sit.

Use the target to teach the dog Out (move away laterally) for agility.

## GO—THE DETAILS

1. Complete all the steps in the Contact Disk behavior in Chapter 2. Pay particular attention to the intensity of this behavior at the outset. We want the dog to be "burning rubber" to get to the contact disk. Review steps 8-13 to make sure you are building in speed and intensity.
2. Change your location every session, gradually working up to being outside on pavement. (Before you start this step, it will be helpful to write down all the places you could easily practice and rank them in terms of distraction level, so that you have a hierarchy.) We'll work on pavement in the initial stages, as we want the dog to know there is a target out there and get to it as quickly as possible. The target is more visible on the pavement than in grass.

*8 correct? Move up a step (and continue to use 8 out of 10 for the remaining steps).*

3.  Gradually add distance, until the dog will run up to 30 feet away from you straight to the target, without veering off path or searching for the target. Remember as you build distance that you will bounce around rather than always asking the dog to go farther each time. Use a toy, food tube or large treat to *reward*, so that your dog does not end up searching for his reward as you build distance. Remember that the dog must also meet your time criteria in order to be marked and treated. If he is not meeting the standard at least half of the time, you may need to adjust your training plan, take a break, and give him slightly more time or work closer. When he meets the standard at least 8 out of 10 tries, increase your average distance.

4.  Add the Go cue. You will chain this cue with the Contact cue in the order "Go"— "Contact," then mark and treat when the dog touches the target. The dog at this point should be very fast to the target. If not, review your shaping plan or video. You may need to take a break, shorten your distance and build up distance again focusing on speed, or try experimenting with a thrown toy rather than a treat. From now on, do not mark and treat the dog for going to the target unless you have given your cues first.

5.  Make a list of places to practice that are not on pavement, and rank them in terms of distraction level. In your first new, non-pavement practice session, you will decrease the distance to 5 feet. Gradually increase the distance, until you have the dog running up to 30 feet away to touch the contact. When you start in a new location, decrease the distance and gradually build it up again each time. If you see searching behavior, immediately decrease the distance until the dog is going directly and quickly to the target, then build up more slowly. Remember you should be bouncing around the distances, not always continually increasing them.

6.  Fade the target. To do this, set the target at least 35 feet away. Give your Go cue, but mark before the dog gets to the target, then toss the toy ahead of the dog. Before each repetition, decide how far the dog must run before he is clicked. It may help to practice this without

your dog a couple of times, to be sure that you are clicking first, then throwing the toy. It may also help to work alongside a fenced area so that you can easily judge the distance and vary it every time. When the dog is reliably racing away from you on Go, you can eliminate the target.

7. Now add equipment. The easiest pieces to start with are jumps. Put a jump directly in front of the dog at an adequate distance and height to allow him to jump cleanly, without knocking the bar. Tell the dog "Go, Over" then mark and toss the toy when he is past the jump. The distance he has to go past the jump will vary, up to 20 feet in a straight line. Speak to your instructor about correct jump heights and the distance between jumps, as well as how far away from the jump your dog needs to start. If you aren't working with an instructor yet, elbow height or lower is sufficient to work on the behavior and keep good speed up, with spacing about 8-10 feet apart. You might also want to read a book such as *Peak Performance* by Christine Zink, DVM to learn more about the physical requirements of jumping.

8. Add more jumps in a straight line, one at a time. Your time standard will now be set with the dog running over intervening jumps. Because the dog is always rewarded some distance past the last jump, he is always ending with a reward. This should keep his speed up, and encourage him to keep taking jumps in front of him until he hears his mark and gets his reward.

9. Start moving behind the dog, first walking, then jogging, and then running.

10. Practice in a variety of environments, with a variety of equipment.

# GO TO A TABLE

We will teach the dog to go a short distance (20 to 30 feet) over a straight line of jumps or series of obstacles and get on a table.

## GET READY

It's very useful to have a dog who is familiar with the table (and knows the cue word for it) and will continue over obstacles in her path to get to it without you, because running in a straight line, the dog will beat you every time.

Tables are used in USDAA, CPE, AKC and UKC competitions. In USDAA, the dog will always do a Down on the table. In AKC, they may do a Down or a Sit, specified by the judge (a Sit on one day of competition weekends, and a Down on the other). In CPE, tables are used to "stop the clock" only, so the dog needs to get on them quickly but will not be required to do another behavior. In UKC the table (or "pause box") requirements are different at each level. For more information on specific requirements for each venue, check their websites.

You'll need to decide in advance whether you would like the dog to automatically lie down, or to wait for a cue to Sit or Down. If you compete in multiple venues, you might want to consider having the dog Down first, and only Sit if you ask for it, since it is more likely the dog will have to lie down or just touch the table rather than Sit.

It would be great if you had a table to practice on, but of course not everyone has a set of agility equipment in their back yard. You can get a reasonable start on this behavior on a couch, then work on the table when you have opportunities at your group class. Another option is to build a wobble (or "Buja") board, a 3ft x 3ft, 3/4 inch plywood board with a painted surface sprinkled with sand, with a hole in the middle. This can be used as a table-like surface, as well as to prep the dog for the teeter.

You may first need to get the dog used to the table. Tables move, especially if you have a large dog, so prep them for it at the outset so they don't get spooked in training. You can work on this by having the dog walk over a low table, feeding meals on it (or part of a meal), and leaving it out for the dog to explore. Let him get on a low table, drop a handful of treats on the table, then have him get off when the treats are gone. Repeat until the dog is eager to jump on the table. If your dog needs more help than this to overcome his hesitancy, please consult with an experienced trainer.

Discuss with your instructor the appropriate table height for practicing. Although in the initial stages you will want the table low to reduce fatigue in the dog, you'll quickly want to bring it to full height or close to it, especially as the dog starts farther away. It takes some effort for a dog to stay on a competition height table hit at a dead run, and you should practice at that height often so that they can manage their approach correctly.

Decide whether to use treats or a toy to reward this behavior. There are advantages to both. If you want the dog to remain on the table (your Stay is poor), treats are the better choice. If you want the dog to be fast to the table, tossing a toy will generate more speed (but is likely to make your Stay iffy).

You'll have to choose which is more important. You can also start with treats and incorporate a toy once you get some stability on the table. This presumes, of course, that your dog likes both equally well!

Set a time standard for this behavior just as you did for the previous one, by timing how long it takes the dog to run a distance and jump on the table. Add a couple of extra seconds to allow for the training situation. You'll need all your usual equipment in addition to a table or facsimile and a couple of jumps.

## SUGGESTED CUES
"Table," "Up," "Hup."

## GO!

1. Put the dog on the table. Cue "Down" and mark and treat the Down.
2. Starting with the dog on the floor, encourage the dog to get on the table by patting it or luring with a treat. Mark and give the treat as soon as he gets on the table, then release the dog to get off.
3. Do another 10 treat session waiting for the dog to get up on the table (without a lure), then marking and treating.
4. Is the dog getting on as fast as you like?  If not, improve the speed before moving to the next step.
5. Add the cue.
6. Chain the Down and Sit to the Table cue.
7. Increase the duration of Down and/or Sit until the dog will remain up to 10 seconds.
8. Gradually increase the height of the table if you need to.
9. Gradually increase your distance from the table, until you can send the dog from five to ten feet away.
10. Incorporate your movements—running to the table, past it, and moving away from the dog, waving your arms, etc.—making sure that the dog will hold position until released.
11. Incorporate jumps and other pieces of equipment that the dog has to navigate before and after the table.
12. Practice in a variety of locations.

## TROUBLESHOOTING

*Dog won't get on the table.*
- Get the dog used to the table movement before continuing.
- Have dog checked for physical problems.

*Dog gets on the table every time she sees it.*
- Behavior is not on cue, go back and review adding a cue in chapters 1-4 for help.
- Make sure other obstacles get rewarded. For example, it's a common mistake not to reward jumping much, which decreases the dog's interest in jumping when there are other "higher paying" obstacles available.
- Don't reward table behavior that you have not cued.

## CROSS TRAINING OTHER BEHAVIORS

Move Out to a table (a lateral movement away from you)—you'll get a lot of use out of this in Gambler/Jackpot runs.

Can you teach the dog to go to the table when you are standing still, with your back to it? If so, you have a dog who is probably able to distinguish different obstacles by their cue name, without relying on your movement. Teach the names of all the obstacles and you'll do very little running when you compete! Not all dogs are able to learn this fine a level of discrimination, but if your dog can locate each of his toys by name, he's probably a candidate!

## GO—THE DETAILS

1. Put the dog on the table (or couch). Cue "Down" and mark and treat the Down. Release the dog but don't encourage him to get off the table, just out of a Down. Remember to vary how long the dog remains in a Down, for up to 10 seconds. Continue at this step until the dog is going into the Down as fast as you would like and remaining there until released. (This may be a sticky step for short coated dogs. It can help to work fast Downs on the ground, then a slick surface, before working on the sandpaper-like surface of a real table.)
2. Starting with the dog on the floor, encourage the dog to get on the table by patting it or luring with a treat. Mark and give the treat as soon as he gets on the table, then release the dog to get off. (We don't recommend Go as your release because the judge will call out "5, 4, 3, 2, 1, GO!") Repeat 3-5 times, then wait and see if the dog will get

up without a lure. (We're using a lure here to get the dog started. Sure, you could shape it, but why? Luring is faster in this case.)

3. Do another 10 treat session waiting for the dog to get up on the table (without luring), then marking and treating the dog when she gets on the table.

4. Is the dog getting on as fast as you like? If not, take a break and come back to it later with a "fresh" dog to see if she is speedier. If she's still not fast (and the issue isn't fear or fatigue or physical limitations), you'll want to improve the speed before moving to the next step. To do this, set a timer for 30 seconds, and see how many times you can get the dog on the table with a treat lure. That is your baseline (30 seconds divided by the number of times on the table = number of seconds to get on the table in one repetition). Now the dog must get up within that amount of time or she does not get marked and treated. When the dog is meeting that criteria 8 out of 10 times (you're keeping records, aren't you?) you can decrease the allotted time. Continue until the dog is as fast as she can be.

*Continue to use 8 correct out of 10 for the remaining steps.*

5. Add the cue. Say the cue just before the dog gets on the table, then mark, treat and release. From this point forward, do not reward the dog for getting on the table without the cue. You'll need to repeat this 50-100 times over several sessions before you move to the next step.

6. Chain the Down and Sit to the Table cue. Work one behavior at a time. Tell the dog "Table"—"Down", then mark and treat the Down, release and repeat. Intersperse that with telling the dog "Table" and marking and treating the dog getting on the table. Pay attention to the dog's speed—you don't want to train a slow response while you're adding complexity to the table performance. Once the dog is quickly lying down on the table, train the Sit in the same fashion. Now intersperse "Table" with "Table"—"Down" and "Table"—"Sit," rewarding the dog for the correct performance. Alternatively, you could chain the Table—Down pattern and require the dog to lie down every time. When the dog starts to automatically lie down after getting on the table, you can drop the Down cue.

7. Increase the duration of the Down and/or Sit until the dog will remain in position up to 10 seconds. You'll be bouncing around different amounts of time rather than progressively increasing it, remember.

8. Gradually increase the height of the table if you need to. Remember that it may take several sessions to get to full height for your dog. Watch carefully for fatigue or reluctance to jump on as you increase the height. You'll want to address any physical issues (weight or condition), or table issues (movement) as they arise.

9. Gradually increase your distance from the table, until you can send the dog from five to ten feet away. If you taught the dog the Go behavior, you can incorporate that here, saying "Go"—"Table"—"Sit", etc. If you didn't teach the Go behavior, you'll still easily get the behavior of running to the table, as long as you build distance slowly and in a variable fashion by bouncing around.

10. Incorporate your movements—running to the table, past it, and moving away from the dog, waving your arms, etc. making sure that the dog will hold position until released. It's very useful in competition to be able to send the dog to the table, then get into position for the next obstacle while the judge does the table count.

11. Incorporate jumps and other pieces of equipment that the dog has to navigate before and after the table.

12. Practice in a variety of locations.

 # DOWN CONTACTS

The dog will run to the end of a contact obstacle (Teeter, Dog Walk or A-Frame) and stop at the bottom with his rear feet on the obstacle, touching with his nose or with both front feet on the ground, waiting until released. *Note*: This is a common performance for the end of the contact. If you prefer another "look" (all feet on the obstacle, for example) just adjust the position of the target accordingly.

## GET READY

The contact zone is the yellow painted area on either side of the three "contact obstacles"—the Dog Walk, A-Frame and Teeter. It ranges in size from 36 to 42 inches depending on what venues you compete in and the particular obstacle. In all venues, the dog must touch in the yellow zone on his way off the obstacle.

This is for safety reasons. So this will be a core behavior for your dog. Training it correctly from the beginning ensures that you won't have to spend time "fixing it" later on. It will also be helpful in competition if the dog will complete the obstacle without you and wait at the bottom until released. This gives you an opportunity to position yourself on the course for a smooth run.

Small dogs, long-backed, and heavy-chested breeds are sometimes taught a running contact, meaning the dog does not stop at the bottom. You can adapt these directions for a running contact by teaching a foot touch rather than nose touch, and by using a thrown toy as a reward. The most difficult part of a running contact is marking the behavior consistently, at the same touch point, so it might help to have a friend deliver the reward so that you can be accurate in marking the behavior. (Make sure the toy is not thrown until the behavior has been marked or you risk teaching the dog to leap off the equipment.) Another option is to purchase a targeting device such as The Powermat™ from 2Mutz (www.2mutz.com) or the Hit It™ from www.cleanrun.com. They both sound a tone when the dog steps on them, and the tone becomes your marker.

Before starting, discuss with your instructor whether you should be working on a foot or nose touch, the specific performance she prefers, or whether you will be doing a running contact with your particular dog. You'll need to adjust the instructions accordingly. If you're working on your own, you get to decide.

We'll start the behavior on stairs. You'll eventually need an A-Frame, Dog Walk, or contact trainer (a portable training obstacle that looks like an A-Frame on one side and a dog walk on the other) in order to work on this behavior. Mandy uses the 3-Way Contract Trainer from NW Agility, www.nwagility.com/agility-contacts.php, which is suitable for small to medium size breeds. It is not stable enough on grass for large breeds. Some trainers will let you rent their field or equipment when they aren't teaching classes, or you may be able to work on this behavior at fun (practice) matches. If not, start saving your pennies, because you'll probably have to invest in at least one piece of contact equipment if contacts are a problem for your dog. As a start, you can use a long board (at least 12" wide by 8 feet long, with a painted sand surface for grip), but the behavior really needs to be transferred to a regular contact obstacle fairly soon in the process, as you are building repetitive physical skills in the dog. If they practice at a low height for too long, they will have difficulty adjusting their body to handle the steeper decline.

We recommend a clicker as a marker, as you'll need the precision. You'll want to practice clicking and delivering a treat directly at the target, without your dog first, until your delivery is smooth on both the right and the left side. As we progress, you'll be slightly behind or in front of the dog when you click (so that he performs the behavior without you being right there) but will need to deliver the food quickly on the target. Practice it!  For a running contact, you'll want to use a reward you can throw.

This behavior is built on the Contact Disk behavior from Chapter 2, with minor variations noted in step 1 below.

We'll give instructions here for a nose touch on the target, the most common method taught, and consistent with the Go behavior from earlier in the chapter. You could also do this with a foot touch, which we recommend if you have difficulty marking the nose touch accurately, if you have a dog who has physical problems with the nose touch or if you want to train a running contact.

## SUGGESTED CUES
"Contact," "Nose," "Bottom," "Hit It," "Plank."

# GO!

1.  Train the contact target from Chapter 2—Contact Disk. As you work this, the dog is touching from 1-3 times before the mark and treat, waiting for his release, and releasing straight off the contact at every step. You will vary your position, working on both the left and right sides, slightly behind and in front of the dog.

2.  Increase distance until the dog will run directly to the target at least 10 feet away, keeping his speed up. Deliver the treat on the target as consistently as you can. Your time standard will be the same amount of time as the dog running that distance plus a second or two for the touch. Only mark and treat touches that meet that criteria or better.

*8 correct? Move up a step.*

3.  Put the target at the bottom of at least two stairs or at the end of a long board flat on the ground. Tell the dog to "Hup" on the stairs (don't use the obstacle cue name, since he's not getting on an obstacle), hold his collar, then cue him

This Beagle is touching the contact disk at the bottom of an A-Frame. Notice that his focus is on the target rather than toward the handler and his front feet are on the ground, rear feet on the equipment.

"Contact," let him go, mark and treat on the target, and release straight off by moving forward as you cue "Release."

4. Continue to add distance to the target by using additional stairs, or use a brick to tilt the long board slightly and gradually work the dog back from the end (make sure it's secure!) Remember to vary your position on the left and right sides, in front and behind the dog. Mark and treat after one to three touches, and deliver your treat on the target. Release straight off.

5. Move to a standard piece of agility contact equipment set at a low height (almost horizontal) or a contact trainer. You can also continue with the long board propped on a sturdy support that gradually increases in height. If you are using the A-Frame, you will put the dog on about 3 feet from the end (using "Hup" rather than the obstacle name) and cue "Contact," mark, treat and release the dog.

6. Continue moving back from the contact target until you can send the dog to it from one end of the equipment to the other. Remember to vary the number of times the dog has to touch, your location in relationship to the dog, and to release the dog straight off the equipment.

7.   Gradually increase the height of the equipment to its full height.

8.   Add the cue name of the obstacle, if you wish: "Frame"— "Contact."

9.   Fade the contact disk by gradually making it smaller. Change to the next smaller disk when the dog is going directly to the disk and holding position until released 8 out of 10 times.

10.   Add distance from the obstacle and vary your position, until the dog will get onto the obstacle regardless of where you are and hold position in the contact zone until released.

11.   Practice running with the dog to the obstacle and past it, with the dog waiting on the contact until released.

12.   Add the remaining pieces of equipment. Start each in a lowered position and work up to full height, as described in steps 5-11. You may need assistance from your instructor with the Teeter so that the dog does not have a scary experience with it moving. She can best advise you how to introduce it. Generally training is started on the A-frame first, then the Dog Walk, then the Teeter, but your instructor can guide you on what is appropriate for your dog, or you may have to work with what you have available.

13.   Practice in a variety of locations.

## KEEP IN MIND

**Use feet instead.** If you want to train the dog to touch with his foot, use one of your foot targets rather than a nose target, and decide whether the dog has to touch with just one or with both feet before starting the training.

**Use your release.** As you work through the behavior, be very careful to use your release word to let the dog move away from the target. It will also be beneficial to release the dog straight off rather than letting him curve back to you. This is important to build early in the behavior, so that the dog goes directly to the target and is encouraged to keep his rear end on the obstacle and front end on the ground, without curving toward you and falling off the obstacle. The easiest way to get a straight exit off the target is to mark and treat the dog, then step forward past the dog as you release, so that he releases in a straight line.

**Be careful with cues.** Do not use your obstacle name to get the dog up on the stairs, the long board or the side of the equipment, as he will be getting up in the wrong direction, then turning around to touch. We don't want him to think this is how he should complete the contact obstacle.

## TROUBLESHOOTING

*Dog does not come straight off the target, but instead turns toward you.*
- Work the long board, releasing straight off and throwing a toy ahead of the target as your reward.

*Dog's rear end comes off the obstacle even though the front end is still touching the target.*
- Work long board, releasing straight off.
- Use a toy thrown ahead of the dog.
- Use exercise pens or other physical props on either side of the long board or obstacle to prevent the dog from coming off. You'll need to make a plan for fading them as well.

## CROSS TRAINING OTHER BEHAVIORS

How far away can you be and still have the dog hit the contact and remain there waiting for a release? How long will he wait on the contact? Can you fool him into getting off by running forward or saying another word besides your release? Can you use a different kind of target to train the dog to touch the up contact?

# 7

# "SOCIAL" TARGETS

There are many target-based behaviors that work well in social environments, whether the dog is doing pet visitations, therapy work, or just visiting with friends. You can even use targets to help a dog learn to work in an assistance capacity.

 ## KISS

The dog will gently touch his nose to a person's cheek where indicated with a finger touch. This is a great use for a nose target. You'll modify the nose touch behavior slightly so that it is a gentle bump on your finger rather than a hard nose poke.

## GET READY

This is an easy behavior to do, requiring only a few steps. It can be taught in a matter of days. You'll want to have this if you do visitations with your dog—many people enjoy a visit with a dog who is affectionate with them. Teaching the dog to bump with his nose rather than lick the person's cheek will be more palatable to most of the people you visit. For those who like it wet and sloppy, use a bit of butter on your fingertip to get the licking behavior (many dogs won't need the extra incentive, but just in case yours does...) If you're training it just for fun, think of the applications for a pet—kissing a child's booboo, touching his nose to wherever you point, etc.

This behavior doesn't require any special targets—the only one you need is already attached to you. We'll use a visual cue (a finger pointing) to ensure that the dog targets the cheek or chin rather than the lips. If you have a dog who has a tendency to lick, pay special attention to step number 3, making sure you mark before the touch to eliminate the lick as much as possible.

## SUGGESTED CUES

"Kisses," "Buss," "Baci," or "Plant It," all in combination with a finger point to the spot you want the dog to kiss.

# GO!

1. Mark and treat the dog for first leaning into, then touching, your forefinger held up. The dog can touch anywhere on your finger initially. Quickly (over just a few sessions) get the dog touching the tip of your finger.

*8 correct? Move up a step*

2. Shape the dog to touch the top of your finger where the fingernail is (remember you'll be placing your fingertip against your face).

3. To get softer touches, mark just before the dog touches the fingertip. Continue at this step until the dog is nosing gently on the fingertip or is just shy of touching it, no matter how excited he is.

4. Over a period of several sessions, gradually move the finger closer and closer to your face. Remember to maintain that soft touch by marking just before the dog touches each time. It shouldn't take many sessions to get all the way to your face.

5. Get the dog touching your finger when it is placed anywhere on your face, left, right or on your chin. If you lose the behavior, try making the change of location more gradual.

6. Add your verbal cue. Say "Kiss" *then* put your finger to your cheek, then mark and treat just before the dog touches.

7. Have other people work with the dog, marking and treating only soft touches. Continue to vary the people you practice with, bringing in young, old and in-between of as many different sizes and shapes as possible.

8. Gradually wean the dog off of the food treat. You'll find this is pretty easy with dogs who enjoy interacting with people and are responsive to laughing and physical contact.

9. You may want to add other variations by having the dog put his feet gently in someone's lap, or having a person hold the dog while getting a kiss, or have the dog sitting in a lap, depending on the size of your dog and the population you'll be visiting.

Mark before the touch (top) if the dog has a tendency to lick (bottom).

## KEEP IN MIND

**Keep it soft.** You may find that the dog is a little rougher at the beginning of your work sessions. Don't worry too much about it, but do continue to mark just before the touch if you need to keep that soft touch.

**Lose the food.** To wean the dog off of food treats, mark and treat every other behavior (Kiss), then only one out of three, then one out of every four or five, and so on, gradually building up the number by bouncing around. Substitute other rewards such as petting if the dog enjoys it. If the dog really prefers treats, mark and treat the occasional Kiss. Make sure it's not just Kisses with you, but with other people also, that get the occasional food reward so the dog continues to be interested in interacting with other people.

## TROUBLESHOOTING

*Dog licks, slobbers on or bites at finger or face.*

- Go back to step 3 and reshape the behavior, marking before the dog touches the fingertip. Stay at this step until the dog is reliably keeping about an inch away from the finger. Gradually (over a period of several sessions) bring the finger back up to your face.
- Try to spread sessions out a lot so that you can practice working with an eager dog and getting that gentle nudge at the outset.
- If the dog is very excited, he may nip instead of kiss. Make sure you test this behavior out on a few willing adult volunteers before bringing in children. It may also help to have the dog work a few practice drills on heeling, sits and downs to take the edge off before you do your visit.

## CROSS TRAINING OTHER BEHAVIORS

Could you train the dog to kiss someone you point at rather than having to touch the finger to face to get the behavior?

 ## VISIT/GO SAY HI

The dog will go to the person indicated, touch their hand, and then interact with them in some way. The behavior also lends itself to greeting another dog if you have a "social wallflower." The dog can target the other dog's rear end (an appropriate dog greeting) and learn some basic social skills.

This is a slight variation in targeting, where the hand target will involve someone other than the owner. Once the dog has touched the other person (or other dog) you'll need to decide what you want him to do—stay and interact, or come back to you. If you're working an approach to another dog, we recommend he come back to you to prevent any problems.

## GET READY

This is a useful behavior for visitations (Animal Assisted Activities or Animal Assisted Therapy), to focus the dog on the other person. Once the dog touches the other person, the dog is reinforced by petting and attention from that person. We'll initially train it having the other person deliver food, but be careful not to stay too long at that step if you want to use this on visits. Otherwise the dog's focus is on the food, rather than the interaction.

Use a clicker to mark this behavior with people to reduce the chance that the dog will turn back to you. For use with touching another dog, you may find it more advantageous to use a bridge word, which will more likely focus the dog back to you and won't be distracting for the other dog.

## SUGGESTED CUES
"Go Say Hi," "Say Hello," "Visit."

## GO!

1.   Teach Touch Nose to Hand in Chapter 2. Once you get the basic touch, have the dog start doing the touch with other people.
2.   Gradually make the positioning of the person's hand more natural, similar to where it would be as they were about to greet a dog.
3.   Add the new cue.
4.   Include a pat on the head, a scratch, kisses, talking to the dog or other interaction after the dog touches, then call the dog back to you to get a treat.
5.   Repeat the previous step with a variety of people that the dog knows.
6.   Repeat the previous step with a variety of strangers, including

Gradually make the positioning of the hands more natural, similar to where they would be if you were greeting a dog.

people that comprise the population you'll be visiting (seniors, schoolchildren, etc.)

7.	Repeat the previous step with small groups of people, so that the dog is going from person to person, using as few treats as possible.

8.	Work in a variety of gradually more distracting locations.

# KEEP IN MIND

**Build confidence.** If you have a dog who is a little worried about greetings, this will make the approach of a person, or an outstretched hand, less intimidating because the dog is anticipating a pleasant interaction.

**Build control.** "Exuberant greeters" will benefit from a target—something specific for them to do when they get to a person. Using a hand target allows you to position that hand low to keep all four of the dog's feet on the floor. Keep the sessions very short for both the above types of dogs to prevent them from getting too nervous or excited. Of course, if your dog is very fearful, or has bitten, nipped, or snapped at other people in the past, you should consult with a qualified trainer to help you work through it.

**Keep it on cue.** Also practice *not* greeting once the dog starts to understand the cue, to make sure that you have control of this behavior. Cue the greeting if the dog does not pull to get to the other person (thus rewarding the dog for waiting for permission to greet).

# TROUBLESHOOTING

*Dog avoids a particular person.*

• If the person is amenable, you might be able to work through this by letting them take the dog for a short walk, playing with a favorite toy, or throwing a ball. But keep in mind during visitations that people may get hurt feelings if they think a dog doesn't like them. Mandy has an "out" sentence if the dog doesn't appear to be enjoying a visit or is avoiding the person, such as "I think she's a little thirsty, do you mind if I take her to get a drink?" or will have the dog do a trick to refocus her. Obviously, if your dog is showing more serious signs of a problem such as growling or snapping, you need to stop the interaction immediately and seek the help of a professional trainer to work through the problem.

• If the dog will touch your hand (and that behavior is strong), you can position yourself next to the person so that you are both facing the dog but the dog will touch your hand. Let the other person give treats for the touch on your hand.

# GO—THE DETAILS

1. We are building this behavior from Touch Nose to Hand in Chapter 2. Once you get the basic nose touch, begin to bring in other people. You may have to start with a person standing directly beside you with their hand held out while you say "Touch." Gradually move the person farther away over several sessions, until they are directly in front of you when you tell the dog to "Touch" and the dog has to turn to them to do so   You can have the person the dog is greeting give or drop a treat on the floor after each touch, depending on how you plan to use this behavior. For AAA/AAT work, alternate between giving the dog the treat, having the other person give a treat, and having the other person pet or interact with the dog, then calling the dog back to you for a treat.

*8 correct? Move up a step.*

2. Gradually make the positioning of the person's hand more natural—held at knee level if they are seated, or by their side or just in front of them if they are standing, for example. Make it similar to where it would be as they were about to pet a dog.

3. Add the new cue. Have the person offer their hand, tell the dog "Go Say Hi-Touch", then mark and treat when the dog touches. Continue to vary where the treats come from with each repetition. You can drop the "Touch" cue when the dog starts to move forward on "Go Say Hi."

4. Include a pat on the head, a scratch, kisses, talking to the dog or other interaction after the dog touches, then call the dog back to you to get a treat. Depending on how much of a social butterfly your dog is, you may want to reward every call back with a tasty treat (i.e., greeting is more fun for him than eating) or only an occasional call with a treat (eating is more fun than greeting). At this step, you are no longer marking the dog for a hand touch, and the dog is rewarded for the approach by attention from the other person. Skip this step if you have a shy dog and just continue with a hand touch, mark and treat (from the other person).

5. Repeat step 4 with a variety of people that the dog knows.

6. Repeat step 4 with a variety of strangers, including people that comprise the population you'll be visiting (seniors, schoolchildren, etc.)

7. Repeat step 4 with small groups of people, so that the dog is going from person to person, using as few treats as possible. Note, if your dog is less interested in visiting with people than in getting treats at this step, you might want to rethink his role as an AAA/AAT dog. Other options might include doing visits with a larger group and performing tricks or showing off costumes instead of doing one-on-one type visits.

8. Work in a variety of gradually more distracting locations.

**Variation to greet another dog**

1. Target another (cooperative, low key) dog with a nose target such as a butter lid or Post It™ note or the finger touch from the previous exercise. A Post It™ note works well because most dogs won't even notice it, but make sure the target dog is okay with it. Put the target on rear end/hip area. Mark and have the dog come back to you for a better treat if he doesn't want to come back, or a treat that's less tasty if he's too eager to come back to you and avoids the other dog.

2. Add the new cue—"Go Say Hi"—"Touch"—mark and treat.

3. Working with the same dog, gradually fade the target until it is gone.

4. Working with another cooperative dog, repeat step 1 with same starting target or a slightly smaller version. Gradually fade that target.

5. Continue working with additional dogs.

6. Take it out in public, working with cooperative dogs out in the real world as you come across them or setting up sessions with friends' dogs.

# HIGH FIVE

The object is to have the dog lift a front paw high to slap your palm. While the dog will probably naturally prefer one foot, you should teach both, working on the preferred foot first.

## GET READY

This is a fun social behavior and makes a great trick if you do visitations with a group. It also easily translates to a wave if you prefer. You'll need to cut your foot target (see Chapter 3) down to a size that you can hold in your hand. If you haven't already done that, do so now. Because you'll be holding the target in one hand, if you choose to use a clicker in the other, your manual dexterity will be put to the test. But you can easily do this using a bridge word as a marker, to leave a hand free. If you have taught a nose touch to your palm, the dog may offer this a lot at first.

Hold your fingers up, palm facing the dog, for the "High Five" cue.

## SUGGESTED CUES

"High Five", "Slap", "Give Me Five."

## GO!

1.  Hold the paw target in your hand, palm up, close to the floor. Mark and treat when the dog touches the target with a front foot. (If the dog has a paw touch on cue, you can use that cue to get the behavior.) Put your target behind your back after each touch, then present it again for the next one.

*8 correct? Move up a step. (Continue to use 8 correct throughout the following steps.)*

2. Staying close to the floor, tilt your hand so it gradually approaches vertical. Your thumb will gradually point up and fingers to the side as you tilt your hand. Mark/treat each touch, and remove your hand and target in between touches.

3. Gradually rotate your hand so that your fingers are pointing up, in a typical high five position.

4. In small stages, raise your hand higher off the floor, maintaining the same orientation, with your palm vertical and the fingers pointing up.

5. When you reach a height where the dog is making a nice high reach to touch, begin to fade the target you are holding. Cut it smaller and smaller, or use a series of smaller targets. To keep your hand open for the High Five visual cue, tape the target to your palm as it gets too small to hold.

6. When the target is less than one inch across, get rid of the target completely and just hold up your empty hand.

7. Add your High Five cue word and wean off the Paw cue word. So you will hold your hand up, say "High Five"—"Paw" and mark and treat when the dog touches. From now on, do not mark and treat the dog if you have not given your verbal cue first. When the dog does the behavior when you say High Five, you can eliminate the Paw cue.

8. Practice at least 10 times in each of 10 different locations, gradually adding more distractions.

9. Mix up the cue with other cues. Occasionally offer your palm in a very different orientation and cue a nose touch.

10. Have the dog practice with other people. You may have to start with the person directly next to you.

# TROUBLESHOOTING

*The dog insists on touching with her nose instead of foot.*

• Make sure your hand is completely obscured by the foot target so that the dog is encouraged to paw at it. Gradually cut it down smaller and smaller as the dog becomes more reliable at offering foot touches.

- Hold your hand, with target, on the floor, so it's easier to touch with a foot than with a nose.
- Put the target on the back of your hand to start, rather than in your palm.
- Ignore nose touches until they stop, and reward anything else.

*The dog won't reach high.*
- The dog may need some time to get her muscles used to the extension. Get a higher reach gradually, one inch at a time. If you get to a point where the dog will not reach higher, this may be the extent of her physical capabilities.

## CROSS TRAINING OTHER BEHAVIORS

Teach the High Five with each front foot. See if you can get the dog to do it while she's standing rather than sitting. Then use it as a high-stepping dance move (in time to the music, if you're really on top of things).

 ## TUG/RETRIEVE

We'll introduce a different type of targeting here, where the dog is asked to do something specific with his mouth. These behaviors are identical in their initial training steps.

For the Tug, the dog will grab an item with his mouth and pull on it. You can use this to teach the dog tug of war, or have him open a door. Tug is great for building confidence in a dog that doesn't play readily. It's also a useful behavior for an assistance dog.

For the Retrieve, the dog will pick up an item with his mouth, and bring it back to you. This behavior has many uses, from being able to easily exercise the dog, to picking up a dropped item to putting away toys to working as an assistance dog to carrying a basket filled with goodies for a visitation dog. With this behavior, the dog may also be working at a distance, with a variety of different "target" items. A retrieve is also used in advanced levels of obedience competitions.

Combine both of them and you have a dog who'll open the fridge and bring you a soda!

## GET READY

You'll need to decide before you start whether you want to teach the Tug or the Retrieve first. Then shape a few other targeting behaviors from throughout the book before coming back to the second variation. Once you shape either of these (or if you have a dog who already has a tendency to bite at things rather than nose them) you'll have to be very quick with your marker to prevent biting from being a "fall back behavior"—one the dog does when he's not getting marked fast enough for nose touches. If you shape them one after the other, you'll really make your life difficult.

For the Tug, you'll need a large diameter piece of rope, consistent with the size of your dog's mouth. The best material for this that we've found is climbing rope, sold at sporting goods stores. For the Retrieve, you'll need a 6 to 8 inch long piece of thick dowel or PVC pipe (about one inch in diameter for a medium size dog).

We recommend a clicker for this behavior—the precision will help you get minor variations in behavior such as a slightly longer pull. Before you start with the dog, practice holding on to the tug rope, toy or dowel, clicking and delivering a treat right on the item, until you can deliver at least 10 treats in one minute.

## SUGGESTED CUES

"Tug," "Get It," "Pull" for tugging. "Fetch," "Take It," "Bring It," for the retrieve.

## GO! — TUG

1. Start by holding the rope. Mark and treat when the dog looks at or leans into the rope. Repeat 5 times.
2. Mark and treat for touching the rope with his nose. Repeat 5 times.
3. Wait for a harder bump with the nose.
4. Wait for an open mouth approach or licking at the rope.
5. Mark and treat when the dog closes his mouth on the rope.
6. Mark and treat when the dog bites down on the rope.
7. Increase biting time.
8. Get a brief bit of the tug behavior.
9. Gradually get longer and longer pulls, by bouncing around.
10. Gradually have the rope be more vertical.
11. Add your cue.

12.     Add other variations as desired.

13.     Take it on the road, playing tug in a variety of locations.

Look for precursors to tugging—notice the Boxer lifts her head slightly (top) before pulling down on the rope (bottom.)

Holding the rope above the dog's head will help you get (and feel) the pulling motion as you work on longer pulls.

## GO! — RETRIEVE

1. Start by holding the dowel. Mark and treat when the dog looks at or leans into the dowel. Repeat 5 times.
2. Mark and treat for touching the dowel with his nose. Repeat 5 times.
3. Wait for a harder bump with the nose.
4. Wait for an open mouth approach or licking at the dowel.
5. Mark and treat when the dog closes his mouth on the dowel.
6. Mark and treat when the dog bites down on the dowel.
7. Increase biting time.
8. Get a longer duration on the bite, by bouncing around, until you have the dog holding on to the dowel for up to one minute.
9. Let go of the dowel after the dog takes it in his mouth (so you are no longer holding it).
10. Extend your hand slightly toward the dog, as if you were going to take the dowel. Mark while the dog is still holding on to the dowel, and treat.
11. Gradually increase hand movement until you are under the dog's chin.
12. Start with the dowel gradually closer to the ground.

13. When the dowel is resting on the floor, gradually fade your hand from the picture.

14. Add your cue.

15. Cue the dog to pick up the dowel, then take a step backward so that the dog has to take a step toward you. Mark while the dog is moving forward. Continue gradually adding steps until the dog is moving a short distance.

16. Transfer the behavior to an object such as a dumbbell or toy (depending on how you plan to use it). Repeat for additional items as desired.

17. Add other variations for your particular use.

# KEEP IN MIND

**Manage mouthing.** Eliminate the option for the dog to mouth either end of the object by covering it with your hands. If you have a piece of rope, it's helpful to hold it with both hands so that it's horizontal initially. With a dowel, hold the end so that the dog is able to place his mouth on the center easily.

**Watch that clicker.** Be careful that the clicker is not positioned so close to the dog's ear that it startles him, especially in the early stages.

**Getting varied responses.** Getting the dog to move to the next step, and not to stop at a step that might have been "it" for another behavior, can sometimes be difficult. To get more varied responses from the dog, try getting multiple nose touches for a couple of sessions. In other words, the dog has to bump with his nose 1, 2 or 3 times before getting clicked and treated. Then try a session selecting out the harder nose bumps (or whatever criteria you are looking for). This technique works for any behavior where you and the dog are "stuck."

**Chaining behaviors.** Each piece of a chain of behaviors must be solid before they are all put together. So if you wanted the dog to put her toys away, you will need train her to go and get a toy, walk with a toy, put a toy over a box, and drop the toy, each separately, then put them together in a chain. Be sure to make a plan for training all the pieces of the behavior in your chain before starting with the dog.

An easy way to put behaviors together is to start from the end and work forward. So, you would start very close to the box, and have the dog pick up the toy and drop it over the box, then gradually add distance to the box. Another way to put the chain together is to put together the adjacent pieces in groupings. So picking up and walking is one group, walking to the box with a toy is another group, and so on. When you have the groupings trained, put them all together in order.

## TROUBLESHOOTING

*The dog spits out the dowel or rope before getting marked.*
- Have someone observe you to be sure that you aren't clicking the dog for letting go (too late!) rather than for a firm grab hold of the item.
- Make sure you don't wave treats around in front of the dog's nose while you're working, which causes many dogs to spit out what they have in anticipation of a tasty treat.

*The dog doesn't seem to be able to move forward with the dowel in his mouth.*
- Try increasing the amount of time the dog is holding the dowel while he is stationary, as well as variations such as pulling on the dowel and marking the dog for holding on tight, or waving your hand around under the dog's chin. When you introduce movement, do it very slowly, only half a step or so increase in each session.

## CROSS TRAINING OTHER BEHAVIORS

Can you teach the dog to go and get all of his toys and put them away with only one cue? (Hint: This is just a long chain of behaviors put together.) How about identifying toys by name?

For a retrieve in obedience, the dog will need to wait while you throw the dumbbell, go get it when sent, then return and sit in front of you until you ask for it. Write out the entire chain and train it from the end (you taking the dumbbell), all the way to the beginning (the dog sitting while you throw the dumbbell).

How many different kinds of objects (think shape, softness, and weight) can you get the dog to pick up?

The latest research shows that dogs are capable of identifying objects by type or modifier such as Soft vs. Hard or High vs. Low. So you could potentially teach the dog to pick up a "hard" item out of a pile of "soft" items. Do a search on the web to find out more about this and experiment with your dog!

# GO—THE DETAILS

## TUG

1. Start by holding the rope with both hands. Mark and treat when the dog looks at or leans into the rope. Repeat 5 times (we don't want to stay too long at the early steps, because we don't want *just* a nose touch).

2. Now the dog must touch the rope with his nose in order to get marked and treated. Remember to deliver the treat as close to the center of the rope as you can. Repeat 5 times.

3. Now wait for a harder bump with the nose. Because you're holding onto the rope, you'll be able to feel it when the dog hits it. Repeat 5-10 times, trying to select out the harder bumps.

4. Wait for an open mouth approach or licking at the rope.

*8 correct? Move up a step. (Continue to use throughout the following steps.)*

5. Mark and treat when the dog closes his mouth on the rope. Be very careful to mark when the mouth starts to close (early or on time) rather than when he pulls away (too late!). This is a good place to have someone observe you or to video sessions to see if you're marking at the correct spot. You'll want to be looking for the precursors to the dog closing his mouth on the item such as leaning forward and opening his mouth so you can time your mark correctly.

6. Mark and treat when the dog bites down on the rope.

7. Get the dog to bite multiple times (1, 2 or 3 times for each mark and treat) for a couple of sessions. Then select out the slightly longer bites and only mark and treat those (this is harder than it might seem!) Again, it's helpful to have an observer look for precursors to the biting motion.

8. Get a brief bit of the tug behavior. Look for the precursors—some dogs move the head up, then down, or move forward then back for a tug or (rarely) they may go side to side. Knowing what to look for will help you time your mark right as the dog is tugging. Holding the rope in your hand will also help you pick out the tugging, because you'll feel it in the rope.

9.  Gradually get longer and longer pulls, by bouncing around. It may also help to hold the rope slightly above the dog's head to get more pulling.

10. Gradually have the rope be more vertical. When it is completely vertical, you can let go of one end and let the dog grab the end if he chooses.

11. Add your cue when the behavior is close to what you want it to look like. Remember it's *cue— behavior—mark—treat* for 50-100 pairings. Then you will only let the dog tug if you have given the cue first, and you will *not* give the cue once every 5 to 10 times and *then* cue if the dog doesn't try to tug. Or, give another cue such as "Sit" and tell the dog to "Tug" as a reward for sitting.

12. Add other variations as desired. For example, you may want to teach the dog to also drop the rope on cue by marking and treating the dog when he loosens his hold. Or you may want to teach the dog to open a door or drawer by pulling on a rope. In order to do this, you'll need to first get the dog used to the movement of the door/drawer, then go for gradually longer pulls. You may have to alter how the dog pulls depending on the size of the dog and how heavy the door is.

13. Take it on the road, playing tug in a variety of locations until the dog is comfortable playing with you wherever he may be.

## RETRIEVE

1.  Start by holding the dowel with one or both hands or place it between your knees if you want your hands free. Mark and treat when the dog looks at or leans into the dowel. Repeat 5 times (we don't want to stay too long at the early steps, because we don't want just a nose touch).

2.  Now the dog must touch the dowel with his nose in order to get marked and treated. Remember to deliver the treat as close to the center of the dowel as you can. Repeat 5 times.

3.  Now wait for a harder bump with the nose. Because you're holding onto the item, you'll be able to feel it when the dog hits it. Repeat 5-10 times, trying to select out the harder bumps.

4.  Wait for an open mouth approach or licking at the dowel.

*8 correct? Move up a step. (Continue to use throughout the following steps.)*

5.  Mark and treat when the dog closes his mouth on the dowel. Be very careful to mark when the mouth starts to close (early or on time) rather than when he pulls away (too late!). This is a good place to have someone observe you or to video sessions to see if you're marking at the correct spot. You'll also want to be looking for the precursors to the dog closing his mouth on the dowel.

6.  Mark and treat when the dog bites down on the dowel.

7.  Get the dog to bite multiple times (1, 2 or 3 times for each mark and treat) for a couple of sessions. Then select out the slightly longer bites and only mark and treat those (this is harder than it might seem!) Again, it's helpful to have an observer look for precursors to the biting motion.

8.  Get a longer time on the bite, by bouncing around, until you have the dog firmly biting the dowel for up to one minute. At this point, you are still holding onto the dowel with one or both hands (or still have it between your knees).

9.  Once the dog is holding onto the dowel readily and for an extended time, you will let go of it after he takes it. Start each repetition by holding onto the dowel, however. Don't worry if the dog drops the dowel when you mark and treat.

10. Now while the dog is holding the dowel, extend your hand slightly toward the dog, as if you were going to take it. Mark while the dog is still holding on to the dowel. Continue to vary how long the dog holds the dowel, for up to one minute.

11. Gradually increase your hand movement, until your hand is directly under the dog's chin. Stay at this step until it doesn't matter how you move your hand, the dog will still hold the dowel until you mark the behavior and give a treat.

12. Now when you start each session, you will start with the dowel held gradually closer to the ground. Move to the next closest approach at each new session, as long as the dog is taking the dowel from you readily, and holding it until you mark and treat, no matter where your hand is positioned once you've let go of the dowel.

13. When the dowel is resting on the floor, gradually make your hand less visible (fade it) by moving it farther away from the dowel. So first mark and treat while you are still holding it, for 5 to 10 repetitions. Then mark and treat while your finger and thumb are touching it.

Then just one finger. Then a finger an inch away, and so on, until you can stand up straight and the dog will take the dowel from the floor.

14. Add your cue, saying it as the dog reaches for the dumbbell. Repeat for several sessions, until you have paired the cue with the behavior at least 50-100 times. From now on, you will not mark and treat the dog if he picks up the dowel without being cued.

15. Cue the dog to pick up the dowel from the ground, then take a step backward so that the dog has to take a step toward you. Mark while the dog is moving forward, so that the dog does not spit the dowel out before you mark. Continue gradually adding steps until the dog is moving a short distance, holding the dowel in his mouth until you mark and treat.

16. Transfer the behavior to another object such as a dumbbell or toy (depending on how you plan to use it). To do this easily, start by holding the new object in your hand and cue the dog to Take It. Quickly work through steps 7-14 with the new item (doing only 5-10 repetitions at each step). Repeat for additional items as desired.

17. Add other variations for your particular use. That might include having the dog sit in front of you holding a dumbbell, go to a toy box holding a toy, or put his paws in your lap holding an item. All of these involve a chain of behaviors that are put together.

# 8

# TARGETS FOR FREESTYLE

Freestyle, or dancing with dogs, is an up-and-coming sport across the country and around the world. You and your dog can compete in person at competitions or via videotape. Different varieties of Freestyle focus on different talent —Heelwork to Music relies on precision teamwork to present a smooth flowing performance without a lot of dance moves or tricks; K9 Dressage is a freestyle variant of Rally-O, where competing teams move through a course (with helpful signs) performing a variety of heeling and dance move exercises; and Freestyle offers flashy costumes, even flashier moves, and musical accompaniment. Go to www.wcfo.org to read more about the details of this competitive venue. Videos of past performances are available for purchase, if you need some ideas on putting together a routine. Local clubs around the country can also provide instruction, practice, and camaraderie.

In this chapter, we'll use our various targets to teach some popular freestyle moves. Spin and weave through legs will use a nose touch, while side-step uses a hip touch.

 ## SPIN

The object is to have the dog turn in tight circles, either in place, or traveling in a larger circle while spinning. Either variation can be useful in a freestyle routine.

Be aware that many dogs are right or left "handed," the same as people. That is, your dog may turn more readily in one direction than the other. It will be easier to teach a spin in your dog's preferred direction first. When that is done, you can go back and teach the other direction. Also, use a little caution—dogs can obsessively spin in circles on their own. If your dog has any tendencies toward this, do not teach this behavior.

## GET READY

You'll need a good solid nose touch to start. Depending on your size relative to your dog's size, you may find that it's easier to use a target stick than a hand touch.

If you don't know if your dog is left or right-pawed, there are a few tests you can do. Place a toy under a low couch and watch which foot your dog uses to paw at it. Have someone hold your dog facing away from you some distance away. Call your dog and observe which way the dog turns to come to you. Or use your target stick to bend the dog to the left and then to the right, and see which is easier.

## SUGGESTED CUES

"Spin," "Circle," "Whirl," with or without a hand signal. If you train both directions, you'll need a second cue for the second direction—"Unwind," "Reverse," "Twist."

## GO!

1. Put the target stick in front of the dog and move it from the dog's nose in an arc clockwise or counter-clockwise (to your dog's favored side) toward his rear end. Mark and treat as the dog follows the stick, tossing the treat so that the dog continues to bend in the same direction to retrieve the treat. Remember to remove the target after each repetition. Start with a minimum arc—say, from six to seven o'clock on the clock face for a dog turning clockwise, with the treat delivered at about eight o'clock.

*8 correct? Move up a step. (Continue to use 8 correct throughout the following steps.)*

2. Repeat step 1, but add another clock number to the arc, so the dog is following the stick from six to eight o'clock, for example.

3. Continue to gradually increase the arc. Once the dog reaches a half-circle (from 6 to 12), you can toss the treat out at about 3 o'clock to continue the turn. Continue to increase the arc until you have a full turn. Once you achieve a complete turn, you have two choices. If you want "Spin" to mean "make

Place the target at 9 o'clock to get the dog to turn, then throw the treat past the dog's nose toward 12 o'clock to encourage more movement

one complete circle and stop," add the cue, fade the target and you're done with this side (see steps 5-8 below). If you want "Spin" to mean "keep turning in circles until I tell you to stop," you need to first work on getting multiple spins, so you'll need one additional step:

4. Use the target to turn the dog through multiple circles before marking and treating. Start slowly—a circle and a half, perhaps—and build up to multiple turns. Do more easy repetitions (1, 1 1/2 or 2 complete circles) than harder repetitions (3, or more) and use a cue word ("Stop" or "Halt") to tell the dog when to stop spinning. Remember to vary how many times the dog has to spin before marking and treating (bouncing around).

5. Add your cue. Say the cue word ("Spin") before presenting the target. You'll no longer mark and treat any spins without a cue.

6. Fade the target. Start making the stick movement smaller, so that you are making a circle in the air above the dog rather than leading the dog with the stick. Gradually make your circles smaller and smaller while the dog continues to spin, until you are no longer moving the stick.

7. Now start collapsing the stick (if you have a retractable or folding version) or holding the stick so less is visible to the dog. Once you've faded the stick completely, you'll be able to use your hand held over the dog's head as your visual cue to keep spinning. If you'd rather not, you'll need a couple of extra sessions to also fade your hand out of the picture.

8. Mix up giving the "Spin" cue with giving other cues your dog already knows.

9. Go back and teach a spin in the opposite direction. Realize that you will likely have to do more repetitions and break the behavior down into more steps to keep the dog working to her "bad" side.

## KEEP IN MIND

**Choose targets carefully.** Using a hand as a target allows you to eliminate several steps since you don't have to fade a target stick. But it may limit your movement more than using the target stick.

**Visualize the time.** Think of a clock face with the dog's nose starting at six o'clock, and use it to visualize how far you are asking your dog to turn at each step. This will help you gradually get more and more of a circle.

## TROUBLESHOOTING

*The dog doesn't follow the target.*
- Make it easier to start. Maybe you have to begin with a head turn, then a body turn, then one step, etc. Also check that you are working in your dog's favored direction first to make your task easier. If you still have problems, go back and strengthen your nose touch behavior (see Chapter 2).
- Try working seated in a chair. Some dogs (especially small ones) get intimidated by someone leaning over or stepping toward them.

*I can't reach far enough to turn the dog all the way around to touch my hand.*
- Go back and teach the dog to touch his nose to a target stick—training should go very quickly. Then use the target stick to teach the spin.

## CROSS TRAINING OTHER BEHAVIORS

Teach your dog to spin on a large doormat before coming in the house, to remove dirt from paws.

Teach your dog to spin while also traveling in a large circle around you.

Teach your dog to alternate spins—one circle in one direction, one circle in the opposite direction.

Could you teach your dog to spin in a circle backwards? What type of target would be helpful for this variation (hint: you'll want to think about other body parts besides the nose)?

 ## WEAVE THROUGH LEGS

## GET READY

You'll need a solid nose touch. With a tall dog you can use a hand touch, but you'll need a target stick touch with a smaller dog. Also, some dogs may be hesitant to pass under the handler, and will need lots of rewards and many small steps to progress during the training.

Train in an area that provides plenty of space for both you and your dog to move around.

## SUGGESTED CUES

"Weave," "Zigzag," "Serpentine," "Eight."

## GO!

1.  Stand as if in mid-stride, with the dog on the outside of your back foot, and put the target under and between your legs, reaching through from the opposite side. Mark and treat for the dog touching the target, and deliver the treat on the same side as the target, slightly in front of where the target was placed.

    *8 correct? Move up a step. (Continue to use 8 correct throughout the following steps.)*

2.  Gradually move the target location so that it is less between your legs and more to the side opposite the dog, moving the dog between your legs. How fast you can move to the next step will depend on how readily the dog will pass underneath you. With a cautious dog, you'll have to proceed more slowly with a lot more rewards at each stage.

3.  Put the target on the side opposite the dog. Mark and treat when the dog has passed completely under you. Give the treat so that the dog turns back to face you, in preparation to go the opposite direction.

Stand midstride with the dog on the outside of your back foot and the hand target between your legs.

4. Work through the first three steps in the opposite direction.

5. Now work both directions, taking a step and switching your target (hand or target stick) to the opposite side after the dog crosses under in one direction.

6. Bounce around three forward steps, having the dog pass through. Do more 1 and 2 than 3 steps.

7. Add your cue.

8. Gradually fade the target. Continue to bounce around the number of steps you take as you are fading the target.

9. Extend the behavior, adding more steps (but doing more repetitions with just a few steps forward).

10. Change your training location and do 10 repetitions. Change locations again. Continue to change locations after every 10 repetitions (and a short break) until you have worked in 10 different locations.

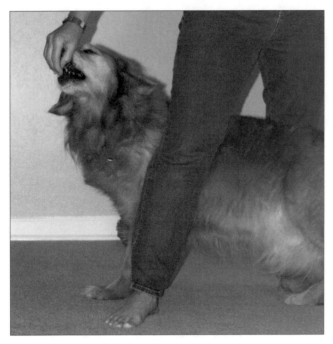

Deliver the treat slightly in front of where the target was and with the dog turned toward you in preparation to go in the opposite direction.

## TROUBLESHOOTING

*The dog shies away from going between my legs.*
- You'll have to take plenty of time to let the dog get used to the idea. Provide a lot of rewards for coming close to your legs, and move to the next stage only when the dog is relaxed. So reward for stretching to touch the target, then taking one step toward it, then several steps, then going near your leg, then the nose under your leg, etc. Work in short sessions. Intersperse with practicing behaviors your dog already does well.

*I'm short and I have a big dog. Can we do this?*
- Yes. You have a couple of options. The dog can learn to crouch to pass under you, the same way she would negotiate an agility tunnel. You can also add a showy high-stepping move, so that either your front or back leg is in the air as the dog passes under you.

## CROSS TRAINING OTHER BEHAVIORS

Vary the details: stand with your legs more than shoulder width apart and have the dog do figure eights around and through your legs.

Stand with your legs shoulder width apart and your dog facing you, have the dog go between your legs from front to back, then pivot on one foot so you are facing the opposite direction, and send the dog between your legs again.

Use a prop such as a cane and have your dog weave between your legs, jump over the cane, take a step forward, and have the dog weave back through your legs.

Have the dog weave backward through your legs—you'll need a different body target for this one!

# SIDE STEP

The dog will step sideways in a crablike motion, keeping his head facing in the same direction and body straight.

## GET READY

You will need a working hip touch so review Chapter 4 if you need to. You may find a clicker useful for this one for precision. It may also help to wear your bait pouch directly over your belly button, to keep your dog's head in a straight line with his rear.

Tape your hip target to a stick so you have a movable target that allows you to easily reach the dog's hip area.

## SUGGESTED CUES

"Sashay," "Cross," "Step."

## GO!

1. Stand with the dog facing you, parallel to your target, with the target about six inches away from the dog's hip. Give your cue for a hip touch as you take a step to the side. Mark and treat as the dog moves his rear foot to touch his hip to the target.

*8 correct? Move up a step. (Continue to use 8 correct throughout the following steps.)*

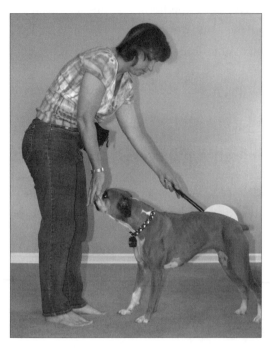

Using a Touch Nose to Hand and a hip target to position the dog in front of you.

2.    Use Touch Nose to Hand to have the dog move his front legs sideways.

3.    Repeat step 1, but now use both your hand target and your hip target to get the dog moving both his front and rear legs at the same time. So present your two targets, say your two cues, and mark and treat for the dog moving sideways.

4.    Continue with step 3, adjusting your targets as necessary, until the dog moves in a nice side-step, with his body straight and nose facing you.

5.    Gradually increase the distance the dog has to follow the target, maintaining a straight body, bouncing around so that some repetitions require fewer steps and some more.

6.    Fade the nose target.

7.    When the dog is stepping sideways well without a nose target, start marking and treating before the dog touches the hip target.

8.  Position the hip target on the dog's other side and go back to step 1. Work through the steps again.
9.  Add your cue.
10. Fade the hip target.
11. Gradually change your position relative to the dog, until you are standing alongside with both of you facing in the same direction. In performance, you might want the dog to sidestep facing you, in heel position, or on your other side. So all these positions should be trained and practiced.
12. Practice various movements—in a straight line, in a curve—in both directions, in different positions relative to your dog.

## TROUBLESHOOTING

*The dog won't keep his body straight.*

- Start with the dog in heel position (next to your leg) rather than facing you. Move toward the dog as you give the cue to touch, so that the dog doesn't have room to curve his body.
- Keep the dog's head facing you with a lure (treat). Give your cue for the hip touch, and move your lure so that the dog will stay straight and move directly sideways.

## CROSS TRAINING OTHER BEHAVIORS

Have the dog side-step from point A to point B while you stay still.

Position the dog behind you and have him shadow your side-stepping movements.

# 9

# TARGETING FOR "SHOW BUSINESS"

Your dog is totally gorgeous or irresistibly cute, right? And he or she ought to be in pictures. . . or commercials. . . or at least calendars. Plenty of dog owners have fantasized about quitting their day jobs and living off the income of their talented canine. We have to tell you that isn't very likely. But you can have a lot of fun (and maybe raise some money for dogs in need) performing at canine charity events and, who knows, other opportunities may come knocking.

You can get started with these behaviors just for your own amusement. But to move on into the entertainment world, you'll need a lot more tricks up your sleeve. You'll need to understand how to train new ones quickly (with targets, of course!) as well as work on keeping the dog in position a distance away, if you're really serious about getting into show biz. You'll also need to find a professional animal handler or agent who is licensed by the USDA or you'll be breaking the law.

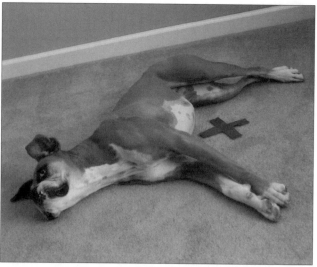

This Boxer is "playing dead" on a taped mark on the floor—a variation of "On Your Mat".

In this chapter we'll use our targets to teach some of the often-used behaviors of the canine acting world. Hug, Sit up, and Bow will use a nose target. Limp and Crawl will need a front foot touch.

 ## HUG

The dog, from behind, will put her head over your shoulder close to your face. This can make a lovely pose for a photograph. Our thanks to Gary Priest—Curator, Applied Behavior, Zoological Society of San Diego—for the idea for this after he described teaching a walrus this for a "photo op."

## GET READY

When you work with your dog behind you, as you will be doing here, you have to keep her engaged or risk losing her attention, so work quickly, make it fun and take frequent breaks.

You'll need a Touch Nose to Hand that's in good working order. Your dog should understand a "stay" or "hold still" cue to help freeze her in position for the photo. If you haven't already taught one, get to it! You'll use it often in this type of work.

You'll have to find the correct height position for your dog relative to you. Large dogs can simply stand behind you as you sit on the floor, but smaller dogs may need to be on a stepstool or couch.

## SUGGESTED CUES

"Hug," "Pose," "Love Me," "Vogue."

## GO!

1. With your dog behind you, hold your right hand over your left shoulder (or vice versa) palm facing the dog and cue your dog to touch. Mark and give the treat where you eventually want the dog's nose to be. If you have trouble holding your hand in the correct position, a contact disk or similar nose target might be helpful.

*8 correct? Move up a step.*

2. Gradually move your hand target to position the dog's chin leaning on your shoulder.

3. Delay your mark just slightly (or use a "stay" cue) to have your dog remain in the chin-on-shoulder position.

Using the Touch Nose to Hand behavior to get the dog to put her chin on your shoulder.

4. Extend the time your dog stays in position. Remember you need to bounce around to do this successfully!

5. Add your cue.

6. Fade your hand target.

## TROUBLESHOOTING

*The dog is reluctant to put her face so close to mine.*

- Break the above steps down into much smaller pieces to give your dog time to get used to the idea of putting her face next to yours. (See the basic target instructions in Chapters 2-4 if you need help with breaking down behaviors.)
- Smear dabs of baby food on your face and have the dog lick them off to get used to approaching your face.

*The dog won't hold the position.*
- Practice a sustained hand touch first, then go back to the over-the-shoulder position. Delay your mark a quarter-second at a time, building up duration very slowly.

## CROSS TRAINING OTHER BEHAVIORS

Use this as a precursor to teaching "Head down," where the dog lies down and puts her head flat on the floor (excellent for having a dog "look ashamed").

 ## SIT UP

The dog will start in a sitting position and then lift her front end up so that her back is straight and upright and her front paws are dangling in the air.

## GET READY

You'll need a strong "Sit" cue and a solid nose touch to your hand.

Some dogs will need to build up their muscles to be able to sit up and hold position. If you need a way to brace the dog, use a corner of two walls or stand so the dog is nestled between your shins.

## SUGGESTED CUES

"Beg," "Pretty," "Put 'em Up," "Say Please."

## GO!

1. Cue your dog to sit, then hold your hand target just above the dog's head so that she has to reach (but not get up out of the sit) to touch. Mark and treat the touch.

*8 correct? Move up a step.*

2. Raise your target a little more, so that the dog has to stretch enough to raise at least one front paw off the ground. Mark and treat. Continue gradually moving your hand target a little higher at each step, until the dog is fully upright. Keep steps small or you'll pull your dog up out of the sit. Try to give the treat while the dog is still sitting up.

Hold your target hand so that the dog's feet come just up off the floor to start with.

3.    Once the dog is fully upright, stay at this step until she is steady and able to hold the position.

4.    Gradually increase duration, by delaying your mark just a fraction of a second at a time as you build up time. Remember to bounce around!

5.    Add your cue.

6.    Fade your hand target.

# TROUBLESHOOTING

*My dog wobbles all over the place.*

- She needs a little body building work. Practice with her butt in a corner, so the walls help hold her steady, or have her sit with her butt between your feet so your legs serve as braces for her.

- Get in some swimming or hill climbing. Both build up the muscles in the rear end and back needed for this behavior.

*My dog keeps getting up out of the Sit.*

- You're trying to move too fast. Break the behavior down into small steps. Move up a step only when your dog is meeting the 8 out of 10 goal.

- Practice sits, mixed up with other behaviors.

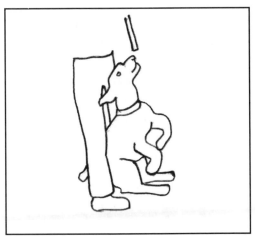

If your dog wobbles, use your legs to serve as braces for her.

# CROSS TRAINING OTHER BEHAVIORS

Combine Sit Up and High Five.

Do a rapid-fire practice mixing up cues for Sit, Stand, Down, and Sit up.

Continue raising your target to teach your dog to "dance" on her hind feet.

 ## CRAWL

The dog remains in a down position or nearly so (some dogs have to raise their butts to accomplish this) and moves forward in a crawl, with his chest along the ground.

# GET READY

You'll need a strong "down" behavior and a foot touch or nose touch. Either one will work so we'll use "target" generically.

This behavior is best practiced on carpeting, or outdoors on grass, to give the dog a good surface grip so he can move more easily.

# SUGGESTED CUES

"Commando," "Sneak," "Creep," "Crawl."

Place the paw target far enough away that the dog has to stretch for it, but doesn't get up from a Down.

# GO!

1.   Cue your dog to Down, put your target in front of the dog so he has to stretch a little to reach it, and cue the Touch. Mark and deliver the treat a little bit in front of the dog's nose.

*8 correct? Move up a step.*

2.   Move the target away slightly as the dog reaches to touch, so that she has to scoot forward just a smidge to reach it.

3.   Move the target a little more, so the dog has to scoot forward a little bit more. Be sure you mark while the dog is still in a Down (or semi-down). Deliver the treat slightly in front of the dog's nose each time.

4.   Move the target farther away from the dog very gradually. Keep your changes in forward position small enough that you don't encourage the dog to get up from the Down.

5.   Once the dog is covering 2-3 feet, mark and treat before the dog reaches the target. So you are marking and treating for

forward movement, rather than a touch (this makes it easier to eliminate the target).

6. Bounce around various distances the dog has to crawl for different repetitions, marking and treating before the dog touches each time.

7. Add your crawl cue.

8. Fade the target.

9. Mix it up with other cues. Alternating "crawl" and "roll over" would be excellent practice. (How would you teach roll over with a target?)

# TROUBLESHOOTING

*The dog will not move forward in a Down.*

- Check with your veterinarian to be sure that there are no physical problems that are making this painful for the dog.
- Teach "bow" first and do the first few sessions of "crawl" working in the "bow" position.
- Break your steps into smaller pieces.
- Try a different target—if a nose target isn't working, try a foot target or vice versa.

*The dog gets out of a Down.*

- You could be moving the target too far, or your dog may need some practice at moving while in a Down. Work under a low coffee table or a chair so the enclosed space helps keep the dog down.
- If you move to the next step too quickly, asking for more than the dog is able to do at that step, he is more likely to get out of the Down.

*The dog raises his butt, then moves.*

- This may be the most comfortable way for him to accomplish moving—give it a fun cue like "Inchworm" and no one will know the difference!
- If you know your dog can crawl without raising his butt (you've seen him do it on his own), work under a low obstacle such as a folding chair or coffee table that will encourage him to keep his butt down.

## CROSS TRAINING OTHER BEHAVIORS

Send the dog to a mark, have him Down, and have him Crawl back to you.

Make it dramatic—have him Crawl a few feet, then stop and put his head down, then Crawl a few more feet.

Put it in a story skit. Cheryl's dog Serling won several talent competitions with a routine as a member of the World War II underground—he said his prayers before leaving on a dangerous mission (target the dog's front feet on your arm, then target his head down between his front legs), rendezvoused with an informant (go to a mark), on his way back he was shot by the enemy and fell over, crawled the rest of the way home, barked out his message, and died. . . then jumped up and took a bow.

Have the dog "swim" by teaching this on a slick floor.

 ## BOW

The dog will assume a play bow position, with her elbows on the ground and her butt in the air.

## GET READY

If you have recently taught Crawl, it may conflict with this, particularly if you've been working on keeping the dog down flat. You'll need a nose touch to your hand or a target stick.

You may want to work sitting on the floor or a low stool, or in front of a mirror, to be better able to see the leg positions you will be rewarding.

## SUGGESTED CUES

"Take a Bow," (if you use "down" to have your dog lie down, "bow" alone sounds too close to "down"), "Applause," "Encore," "Curtsey."

## GO!

1. Standing in front of your dog, present your target low and between the dog's front legs, so the dog has to stretch down to touch with her nose.

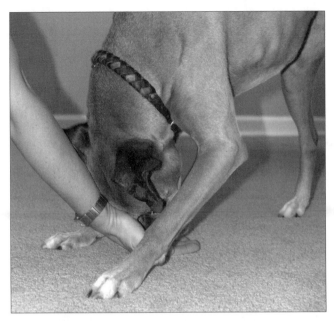

Hold your hand palm up, between the dog's front legs and slightly toward the rear end, to get a bend in the elbows for the beginning of "Take a Bow."

*8 correct? Move up a step.*

2.   Move your target between the dog's front legs, angled in from the front, in a position that makes the dog lower her front end rather than just her head to touch. Mark the leg movement (i.e., a slight bend of the elbow).

3.   Move your target to create more leg movement. Mark the movement, before the dog touches, if possible.

4.   When the front end is nearing the ground, be careful to mark quickly and let the dog up, not giving the rear end a chance to go down.

5.   Once you get the forelegs fully on the ground, begin to work on duration. Be careful to make your delay very short initially. The more you can avoid the dog collapsing into a Down, the better.

6.   Gradually increase duration.

7.   Add your cue.

8.   Fade the target.

9.      Gradually stand up straight, and/or move yourself around beside your dog, depending on if you will both be bowing or if you just want the dog to Bow to you.

## TROUBLESHOOTING

*The dog doesn't bend her front legs, she backs away.*
- Work with the dog backed into a corner so that she can't move away.
- Present the target under her body and behind her front leg so you block her moving backward (but be sure to let the leg bend).

*The dog immediately collapses into a Down.*
- Mark and release the dog quickly from the Bow (before she lies down). You may have to start with just a slight elbow bend and build from there.
- Place your free hand just under the dog's stomach as a gentle reminder to keep the back end up. You'll need to fade this assistance later.
- Try turning your hand palm down, so the dog has to turn her head and lean down to touch. This will often get the initial elbow bend for you to mark and treat.

# LIMP

The dog holds up one front foot and moves forward on three legs, as if injured.

## GET READY

We will be using a foot touch, so if you have not taught one, do so before beginning these instructions.

You may want to tape your foot target to a dowel so you can get it into position more easily. A clicker will probably prove helpful for this behavior. Remember how to hold a clicker and a target stick from Chapter 2. This can be a challenging behavior because an uninjured dog finds it awkward to move forward while holding a foot up.

## SUGGESTED CUES

"Are you Hurt?" "Poor Puppy," "Medic," "Owie," "Got a Boo-Boo?"

# GO!

1. With your dog in a standing position, put your foot target in front of the dog and cue the dog to Paw. You don't want an extremely high touch for this—just enough so the forearm is roughly parallel to the floor. You may have to start with a lower touch and build up.

*8 correct? Move up a step. (Continue to use 8 correct throughout the following steps.)*

2. Gradually move your target more under the dog's body, so that the dog lifts the leg but tucks it back under himself.
3. Work on duration of holding the foot up, delaying the mark a little at a time, until the dog will hold it for approximately 5 seconds.
4. Have the dog lean forward by moving your foot target forward slightly.
5. Move your foot target slightly more forward and wait for any movement of any other foot while one front foot is being held up. It will nearly always be a back foot that moves, so watch carefully and be ready to mark.
6. Wait for movement of two feet while one front foot is held up. It will almost certainly be the two back feet that move.
7. Keeping your sessions very short, wait for movement of the front foot still on the ground. This is usually the hardest step for the dog to accomplish. If you get any kind of hop or shuffle or definite attempt to move that foot, mark and treat. Gradually build up to more and more definite forward move ment, until you get a step or two.
8. Bounce around different numbers of limping steps.
9. Add your cue.
10. Mix it up with other cues or chain it together in a pattern of behaviors—going from Limp to Crawl or Crawl to Limp can be an effective part of a story-telling routine.

# TROUBLESHOOTING

*I can't get the dog to stand.*
• Use a Touch Nose to Hand to position the dog in a stand.

*My dog freezes and won't move anything while holding the foot up.*
- Work through steps 4 through 6 again to get the dog moving, and be very observant in watching for foot movement of any type (forward, up or side to side!) in step 5.
- Use your hand as a nose target, putting it just far enough in front of the dog to force him to lean while he's holding up the front foot and mark and treat that. Add a little more distance and a back foot should move.

## CROSS TRAINING OTHER BEHAVIORS

Can your dog back up in "limp" position?

Make up routines rather than just doing isolated tricks. Put the behaviors together in a chain and write little stories around the behaviors your dog can do.

Use hand signals only for all your behaviors in this chapter (this will be necessary if you use the dog in film work).

Get together with friends and do group performances.

# RESOURCES

## EQUIPMENT/SOURCES MENTIONED IN THE BOOK

**Treat & Train** – www.nerdbook.com/sophia/treat&train
**Easy Walk Harness** – www.premier.com
**Tug-N-Treat** – www.cleanrun.com
**Powermat** – www.2mutz.com
**Hit It** – www.cleanrun.com
**3-Way Contact Trainer** – www.nwagility.com/agility-contacts.php
**Click Stick II** – www.legacycanine.com

## ORGANIZATIONS

**USDAA agility** – www.usdaa.com
**NADAC agility** – www.nadac.com
**AKC agility** – www.akc.org
**UKC agility** – www.ukcdogs.com
**CPE agility** – www.k9cpe.com
**Freestyle** – www.worldcaninefreestyle.org
**Deaf dog resources** – deafdogs.org/training/vibratrain.php

## WEBSITES

**www.clickandtreat.com** – Gary Wilkes' site – books, videos, supplies, training information

**www.clickersolutions.com/clickersolutions/cshome.htm** – A popular clicker list

**www.hsnp.com/behavior/** – Bob Bailey's site

**www.click-l.com/faqs.html** – A popular clicker list

**www.apdt.com** – Association of Pet Dog Trainers

**www.iaabc.org** – International Association of Animal Behavior Consultants

**www.dogwise.com** – Dogwise, a top source for books, videos, toys

**www.writedog.com** – Cheryl's website, where you can ask questions, if you have some left over

**www.clickertraining.com** – Karen Pryor's website, with a variety of tools and resources

## RECOMMENDED READING — Available at www.dogwise.com

*Quick Clicks* by Cheryl S. Smith and Mandy Book – clicker training, step by step, with more helpful exercises and games

*Clicker Journal* – order at www.clickertrain.com (includes articles on training a variety of species)

*Behavior Modification, What It Is and How to Do It* by Garry Martin and Joseph Pear – all the scientific details in an easy-to-understand book

*Don't Shoot the Dog* by Karen Pryor – the original book that brought clicker training to the attention of dog trainers

*Click for Joy* by Melissa Alexander – answers to common questions about clicker training

*The Power of Positive Dog Training* by Pat Miller - clicker basics, with a 6-week puppy training course

*Ruff Love* by Susan Garrett – a program to put you in charge and motivate your dog to work

## RECOMMENDED VIEWING — Available at www.dogwise.com

*Train Your Dog, The Gentle Positive Method* DVD featuring Nicole Wilde and Laura Bourhenne – clicker training in action

*Puppy Kindergarten Video* featuring Corally Burmaster – clicker basics

*Take a Bow Wow Video* featuring Virginia Broitmanan and Sheri Lippman – tricks taught with positive methods

*The How of Bow Wow DVD* featuring Virginia Broitmanan and Sheri Lippman – foundation skills with clicker training.

# RECORDING SHEET #1

## TRACKING CORRECT RESPONSES (8 CORRECT, MOVE UP A STEP)

DOG NAME _____  BEHAVIOR _____

LOCATION _____  START DATE _____

STEP _____

Comments:

| DATE/TIME | GOAL/SPECIAL NOTES | # CORRECT | SESSION TIME | MOVE UP? |
|-----------|--------------------|-----------|--------------|----------|
|  |  | /10 |  | Y / N |
|  |  | /10 |  | Y / N |
|  |  | /10 |  | Y / N |
|  |  | /10 |  | Y / N |
|  |  | /10 |  | Y / N |
|  |  | /10 |  | Y / N |
|  |  | /10 |  | Y / N |
|  |  | /10 |  | Y / N |
|  |  | /10 |  | Y / N |
|  |  | /10 |  | Y / N |
|  |  | /10 |  | Y / N |
|  |  | /10 |  | Y / N |
|  |  | /10 |  | Y / N |
|  |  | /10 |  | Y / N |
|  |  | /10 |  | Y / N |
|  |  | /10 |  | Y / N |
|  |  | /10 |  | Y / N |
|  |  | /10 |  | Y / N |

*TRACKING SPEED OF RESPONSE*

DOG NAME _____  BEHAVIOR _____

LOCATION _____  START DATE _____

STEP _____

Comments:

| DATE/TIME | GOAL/SPECIAL NOTES | # CORRECT | GOAL # | TIME ALLOTED | MOVE UP? |
|---|---|---|---|---|---|
| | | | | | Y / N |
| | | | | | Y / N |
| | | | | | Y / N |
| | | | | | Y / N |
| | | | | | Y / N |
| | | | | | Y / N |
| | | | | | Y / N |
| | | | | | Y / N |
| | | | | | Y / N |
| | | | | | Y / N |
| | | | | | Y / N |
| | | | | | Y / N |
| | | | | | Y / N |
| | | | | | Y / N |
| | | | | | Y / N |
| | | | | | Y / N |
| | | | | | Y / N |
| | | | | | Y / N |
| | | | | | Y / N |

## AUTHOR BIOGRAPHIES

**Mandy Book** has been an instructor and author for over 19 years. Her career began in puppy classes with her first dog, Tonka. After assisting the instructor for 6 months, she was asked to teach and has never looked back. In 1989, she started her own successful training company, Oz Training, which she owned and operated for 10 years. She sold Oz in 1999 but continues to teach as well as offering private training to clients. She is a co-author of the highly successful book *Quick Clicks* and writes frequently for *Clean Run*, a monthly magazine for agility competitors. She has successfully trained humans, cats, chickens and dogs, and specializes in clicker training in both group classes and her private practice. In 2004 she became a Certified Pet Dog Trainer, one of only 500 in the US. Her work with the Humane Society of Silicon Valley, Canine Companions for Independence and in media work with dogs has given her experience with a wide range of temperaments and learning rates in both dogs and people. She competes in agility, and does pet visitations in local classrooms and at senior care facilities with her Delta-certified dogs. She currently lives with 2 Boxers, a Golden Retriever and her husband in San Jose, California.

**Cheryl S. Smith** has been studying dogs for 25+ years. Cheryl joined the Association of Pet Dog Trainers as a founding member, and has attended many of their educational conferences and lectured at one. She is now also a Certified Dog Behavior Consultant with the IAABC, and a member of the National Association of Science Writers.

Cheryl began writing for magazines, and appeared frequently in Dog Fancy, Dog World, and the AKC Gazette. She wrote columns for OffLead, the Pet Gazette, and the Dog Writers Association newsletter. Her work has also appeared in Dog Watch, Pet Life, You and Your Dog, and Veterinary Practice News. Cheryl became a book author in 1991, and has regularly produced dog books ever since (see her website www.writedog.com for titles):

Cheryl has been honored to receive multiple Dog Writers Association Maxwell medallions for excellence in dog writing, the Eukanuba award for writing on canine health, The PetSafe award for best writing on training, the ProPlan President's award (the DWAA's "best in show"), and the Cat Writers Association Muse medallion for article writing. After moving to Washington, she began hosting her own radio show, PetSmith, on station KONP.

Cheryl is an international lecturer, having spoken at the Tufts Animal Expo, the Purina Nutrition Forum, the Animal Fanciers Club in Japan, Van Dusen Gardens in Canada, and garden shows in Seattle, Boston, White Rock, and Bainbridge Island. She presented a weekend clicker seminar with co-author

Mandy Book, was the keynote speaker at the ADMA mushers convention in Fairbanks, and will teach at the WCFO Freestyle national conference.

Cheryl teaches dog training class for Terry Ryan's Legacy Canine. She attended Bob Bailey's chicken camp in Arkansas, and taught at Legacy's Chicken and Dog Camp in Washington. She is an evaluator for the Delta Society's Pet Partners program and a judge for the AKC Canine Good Citizen program. She is currently practicing agility and herding and writing regularly for Clean Run magazine. Cheryl lives in Port Angeles, Washington.

# INDEX